# VEGAN
# AFRICA

# VEGAN
# AFRICA

## PLANT-BASED RECIPES FROM
## ETHIOPIA TO SENEGAL

### MARIE KACOUCHIA

THE EXPERIMENT

NEW YORK

VEGAN AFRICA: *Plant-Based Recipes from Ethiopia to Senegal*
Copyright © 2021 by Éditions La Plage
Translation copyright © 2022 by The Experiment, LLC

Originally published in France as *Cuisines d'Afrique* by Éditions La Plage in 2021. First published in English in North America in revised form by The Experiment, LLC, in 2022.

The Experiment, LLC
220 East 23rd Street, Suite 600
New York, NY 10010-4658
theexperimentpublishing.com

THE EXPERIMENT and its colophon are registered trademarks of The Experiment, LLC. Many of the designations used by manufacturers and sellers to distinguish their products are claimed as trademarks. Where those designations appear in this book and The Experiment was aware of a trademark claim, the designations have been capitalized.

The Experiment's books are available at special discounts when purchased in bulk for premiums and sales promotions as well as for fundraising or educational use. For details, contact us at info@theexperimentpublishing.com.

Library of Congress Cataloging-in-Publication Data available upon request

ISBN 978-1-61519-900-6
Ebook ISBN 978-1-61519-901-3

Cover and text design by Jack Dunnington
Photographs and styling by Fatou Wagué
Additional styling by Marie Kacouchia
Editorial direction by Céline Le Lamer
Editorial operations by Wendy Gobin
Translation by Kiley Malloy

Manufactured in China

First printing November 2022
10 9 8 7 6 5 4 3 2 1

*To my dear parents*

# AKWAABA!

## BIENVENUE!

Welcome!

———

My name is Marie, and I'm a young Parisian woman who has juggled the cultures of two different countries— France and Côte d'Ivoire (Ivory Coast)—since childhood. Cooking is my passion and, with this book, I hope to share my unique cultural experience with others.

There's an ancient African proverb that says, "If you don't know where you're going, remember where you came from." As immigrants and travelers, from Africa or elsewhere, we draw from the culture of our motherland and from the cultures of the countries that welcome us. The cuisine of immigrants, I like to say, is mixed by nature.

But I don't see this as a flaw. In fact, it's the opposite: Cultural diversity is quite a force. It makes me who I am: a strong woman full of depth and character. It feeds my creativity and pushes me to see the world with curiosity and an open mind.

The kitchen is my bridge between France and Côte d'Ivoire, two nations with strong culinary pride. In both countries, food brings people together.

The recipes in this book are inspired by advice from my mother, Marie-Madeleine: "We cook with our hearts or not at all." Making food is a great way to share parts of ourselves and our cultures. So I encourage you to clear the table, set out beautiful dishes, and take the time to appreciate the beauty of the ingredients in this book.

# CONTENTS

*Introduction:* YOU ARE WHAT YOU EAT . . . . . . . . . . . . . . . . . . . . . . . . . . . . . . . . . . . . . . . . . . .1

## SAUCES

Ivorian Vinaigrette (Virgin Sauce) . . . . . . . . 8

Tomato Sauce . . . . . . . . . . . . . . . . . . . . . . . . . . 11

Satini Cotomili (Cilantro Chutney) . . . . . . . 11

Mango-Chile Sauce . . . . . . . . . . . . . . . . . . . . . 12

Nokoss Vert
(Senegalese Green Pepper Paste) . . . . . . . . . 14

Peri-Peri Sauce . . . . . . . . . . . . . . . . . . . . . . . . . 15

## SNACKS

Crunchy Spiced Chickpeas . . . . . . . . . . . . . . . 18

Roasted Sweet Potato Hummus . . . . . . . . . . 21

Peanut Hummus . . . . . . . . . . . . . . . . . . . . . . 22

Sweet Pepper and Corn Cakes . . . . . . . . . . . 24

Red Bean Cakes . . . . . . . . . . . . . . . . . . . . . . . .25

Sweet Potato and Ginger Loaf . . . . . . . . . . . 27

Plantain Beignets . . . . . . . . . . . . . . . . . . . . . . 28

Spiced Popcorn . . . . . . . . . . . . . . . . . . . . . . . . 31

Alloco (Fried Plantains) . . . . . . . . . . . . . . . . .32

Paprika-Spiced Plantain Chips . . . . . . . . . . .35

Sweet Potato Fries . . . . . . . . . . . . . . . . . . . . . 36

Chapati (East African Flatbread) . . . . . . . . 38

Sweet Bread . . . . . . . . . . . . . . . . . . . . . . . . . . . .41

Injera (Ethiopian Flatbread) . . . . . . . . . . . . 42

Coco Bread . . . . . . . . . . . . . . . . . . . . . . . . . . . .43

Savory Mauritian Crêpes . . . . . . . . . . . . . . .45

# STARTERS

Roasted Eggplant with Tamarind . . . . . . . . 49

Sweet Potato Salad with Mixed
Baby Greens and Cashews . . . . . . . . . . . . . 50

Red Cabbage Salad with
Mango and Peanuts . . . . . . . . . . . . . . . . . . .52

Mango, Avocado, and Radish Salad . . . . . . .55

Cumin-Spiced Orange and
Chickpea Salad . . . . . . . . . . . . . . . . . . . . . . 56

Kachumbari (East-African Tomato and
Onion Salad) . . . . . . . . . . . . . . . . . . . . . . . . 56

Fonio and Papaya Salad . . . . . . . . . . . . . . . 57

Red Cabbage Salad with
Mango and Raw Okra . . . . . . . . . . . . . . . . 58

Fresh Pineapple Salad . . . . . . . . . . . . . . . . .61

Roasted Cauliflower with
Peanut-Ginger Sauce . . . . . . . . . . . . . . . . . 62

Cauliflower Tabbouleh with Pistachio and
Lemon Confit . . . . . . . . . . . . . . . . . . . . . . . . 63

Cassava Tabbouleh with Radishes
and Herbs . . . . . . . . . . . . . . . . . . . . . . . . 64

Vegetable Pastels . . . . . . . . . . . . . . . . . . . . . 66

Creamy Corn Soup with Peanuts . . . . . . . . 67

Creamy Roasted Tomato
and Pepper Soup . . . . . . . . . . . . . . . . . . . . 68

Creamy Carrot-Ginger Soup . . . . . . . . . . . . .71

Creamy White Bean Soup with Crispy
Coconut Bacon . . . . . . . . . . . . . . . . . . . . . 72

Chilled Watermelon, Tomato,
and Mango Soup . . . . . . . . . . . . . . . . . . . . .73

Sopa de Amendoim
(Angolan Peanut Soup) . . . . . . . . . . . . . . . .75

Rwandan Vegetable Soup . . . . . . . . . . . . . . 76

# MAIN DISHES

Plantain and Eggplant Stew . . . . . . . . . . . . 80

Cauliflower Yassa with Olives . . . . . . . . . . . 83

Grilled Squash with Harissa . . . . . . . . . . . . . 84

Sautéed Spinach and Mushrooms with
Plantains . . . . . . . . . . . . . . . . . . . . . . . . . . . 87

Grilled Vegetable Wraps . . . . . . . . . . . . . . . 89

Creamy Avocado Risotto . . . . . . . . . . . . . . . 90

Millet with Roasted Tomatoes . . . . . . . . . . .91

Potato Stew with Olives . . . . . . . . . . . . . . . 92

Chakalaka (South African Relish) . . . . . . . . 94

Sweet Potato and Kidney Bean Stew . . . . . 97

Egusi Stew (African Pistachio Stew) . . . . . 99

Yam Akpessi (Ivorian Eggplant and Yam) . . 100

Atakilt Wat (Ethiopian Cabbage, Potatoes,
and Carrots) . . . . . . . . . . . . . . . . . . . . . . . 103

Red Red (Ghanian Red Stew) . . . . . . . . . . 104

Bobotie (South African Casserole) . . . . . . 106

Gari Foto (Togan Cassava with Tomato) . 107

Yassa Burger . . . . . . . . . . . . . . . . . . . . . . . . 108

Githeri (Kenyan Corn and Bean Stew) . . .110

Vegetable Mafe (Malian Peanut Stew) . . . . 113

Gratitude Bowl . . . . . . . . . . . . . . . . . . . . . . .114

Key Sir Alicia (Ethiopian Beet
and Potato Stew) . . . . . . . . . . . . . . . . . . . .117

Irio (Potato, Pea, and Corn Purée) . . . . . . .118

Etor (Ghanaian Banana Purée) . . . . . . . . . .121

# RICE

Vermicelli Rice with Spinach
and Cashews . . . . . . . . . . . . . . . . . . . . . . . . 125

Rice with Green Lentils and Onion . . . . . . 126

Geelrys (South African Yellow Rice
with Raisins) . . . . . . . . . . . . . . . . . . . . . . . 128

Jollof Rice . . . . . . . . . . . . . . . . . . . . . . . . . . . 130

Pilau Rice . . . . . . . . . . . . . . . . . . . . . . . . . . . 131

Atassi (Beninese Rice and Beans) . . . . . . . . 132

# DESSERTS

Mango-Chile Compote . . . . . . . . . . . . . . . . 136

Chilled Mango-Basil Soup . . . . . . . . . . . . . . 136

Coconut-Lemongrass Muffins . . . . . . . . . . . 137

Chocolate Mousse . . . . . . . . . . . . . . . . . . . . 139

Coconut Rice Pudding . . . . . . . . . . . . . . . . 140

Banana–Peanut Butter Ice Cream . . . . . . . 143

Chocolate-Ginger Muffins . . . . . . . . . . . . . 144

Peanut-Date Cookies . . . . . . . . . . . . . . . . . 146

Plantain Pancakes . . . . . . . . . . . . . . . . . . . . 149

Coconut-Lime French Toast . . . . . . . . . . . 150

# DRINKS

Date-Infused Cashew Milk . . . . . . . . . . . . . 154

Spiced Hot Chocolate . . . . . . . . . . . . . . . . . 157

Coconut-Mango Milkshake . . . . . . . . . . . . 158

Basil Bissap (Hibiscus Tea with Basil) . . . 160

Lemongrass Lemonade . . . . . . . . . . . . . . . . 163

Kinkeliba-Mint Iced Tea . . . . . . . . . . . . . . 164

MENUS FOR ALL OCCASIONS . . . . . . . . . . . . . . . . . . . . . . . . . . . . . . . . . . . . . . 166

ACKNOWLEDGMENTS . . . . . . . . . . . . . . . . . . . . . . . . . . . . . . . . . . . . . . . . . . . . 169

INDEX . . . . . . . . . . . . . . . . . . . . . . . . . . . . . . . . . . . . . . . . . . . . . . . . . . . . . . . . . . 171

ABOUT THE AUTHOR . . . . . . . . . . . . . . . . . . . . . . . . . . . . . . . . . . . . . . . . . . . . 180

# YOU ARE WHAT YOU EAT

This book is both an invitation to travel through food and an ode to cross-cultural cooking and diversity. Inspired by my childhood in Côte d'Ivoire (Ivory Coast), I wanted to create recipes that are both vegan and healthy. These recipes are inspired by my cherished memories of my carefree childhood years.

Writing them, I was transported back to Grand-Bassam, a town my family and I would often visit. I imagined my feet in the sand as I tasted different dishes, each more delicious than the last. I saw myself as a child again, coming home from school with my brothers and heading straight to the kitchen, to see my mother cooking Alloco (Fried Plantains, page 32) at the stovetop. I remember the brightly colored markets, the stalls overflowing with mouth-watering fruits and vegetables. This is where I hope my recipes will take you.

The recipes are also influenced by my life in Paris which, though much more hectic, is still dedicated to making and eating quality food. They're easy to make and the ingredients are easy to find at your local supermarket, farmers' market, or specialty grocery store.

## REEXAMINING AFRICAN CUISINES

There isn't just *one* African cuisine; there are many African cuisines, each containing their own key ingredients, emblematic recipes, and treasures for the taste buds. To speak of one African cuisine is simplistic.

There's also a stereotype, believed by many in African diasporas, that African dishes are unhealthy. This isn't true. There are certainly heavy, filling dishes in African cuisines, but the ingredients themselves are not "bad food." They can be cooked in very healthy ways. Like most cuisines, African dishes are more or less balanced. In this book, we'll discover their riches.

It's also not true that all African recipes have to simmer for hours on end. Many are simple, require only a few ingredients, and they're ready in the blink of an eye! Stereotypes like these are also common within the African diaspora, so many immigrants reserve dishes from their childhood for special occasions only. I hope that the recipes in this book will help remove these stereotypes.

## WHAT DOES IT MEAN TO BE VEGAN?

Being vegan means excluding all animal products from your diet. It's not only a dietary decision but also a way of life founded on respecting every living being. As with any diet, the key is balance. A balanced vegan diet includes grains, fruits, vegetables, nuts, and legumes. It shouldn't be deficient in anything except vitamin B12, which can be taken in supplement form. If you haven't yet made the change to a vegan diet, I'd suggest consulting a nutritionist or other trusted health professional.

## WHY WRITE A BOOK ABOUT VEGAN FOOD?

One of my reasons for writing this book is to show that moving toward a plant-based diet doesn't have to be boring or restrictive. For me, it's the opposite: Being vegan makes me a more creative cook. I hope that, with this book, you'll find the resources you need to reinvent your daily diet and spark your own curiosity and creativity.

I also wanted to write a book of vegan African recipes to combat preconceived ideas about African food. While it's true that Africans often place meat at the center of their plates, delicious, vegan African dishes have existed for centuries. Don't forget that our ancestors didn't always eat meat!

## A HOLISTIC APPROACH TO NUTRITION

Why do we eat, anyway? First and foremost, we eat to live! We need to have enough energy for our bodies to work properly. Eating is a vital part of our daily routine, but these days, we tend to set aside less and less time for it. This has consequences in many areas of our lives—food affects our health, of course, but eating is a political act, and the choices we make have an ecological, social, and environmental impact.

Adopting a holistic approach to nutrition is about trying to reunite yourself with a diet that nourishes both the body and the soul, while respecting the planet and the beings that inhabit it. In a more concrete sense, a holistic approach attempts to replace processed foods with whole ingredients. It means knowing what foods are in season, choosing organically grown fruits and vegetables when possible, and supporting local farmers and businesses.

It doesn't have to be perfect, but it's truly possible to eat well and with enjoyment, while also doing your part to make the world a better, kinder place.

## SIMPLE BUT DELICIOUS FOOD

For these recipes, I've chosen simple ingredients that are as close to their original forms and as unprocessed as possible. These ingredients are often humble. I find pleasure in making them sublime—doing more with less. This isn't always easy, as it requires the investment of both time and energy in the kitchen. But the result is well worth it.

## THE VEGAN AFRICAN PANTRY

Here are the ingredients I always have on hand. If you keep these in your pantry, you'll be able to improvise recipes with African flavors at any time. They can all be found at most grocery stores, but if you can't find them there, don't worry! You can always order them online.

## Fruits and vegetables

Fresh fruits and veggies—the esssential part of this cookbook—should make up close to 50 percent of your diet. I encourage you to play with different colors and varieties when making my recipes.

Like we do in Abidjan, don't hesitate to wander between stalls of a farmers' market or chat with your local greengrocers to learn their secrets. In Côte d'Ivoire, the market is a social scene. We chat with each other, haggle for better prices, and carefully choose the freshest vegetables for our meals.

In Paris, it's a little different: I love strolling through the local shops and discovering new products. It fuels my creativity, like magic!

When picking fruits and vegetables, try to choose those that are organic and in season. If that's not possible, opt for frozen options. In the summer, you can buy your favorite fruits and vegetables in season and then store them in the freezer so that you never run out.

## Grains and Legumes

**SEEDS:** The bearers of life, they are one of the staples of a vegan diet. Seeds are rich in proteins and essential micronutrients (vitamins, minerals, and enzymes). Some (like alfalfa, chickpea, parsley, radish, sesame, sunflower) can also be sprouted to maximize their benefits.

**RICE:** Though rice originated in Asia, it is a staple ingredient in most African cuisines. We often eat white rice (in Jollof Rice, page 130, for example), which has a unique texture as the grains are broken during the harvesting and cleaning processes. Brown rice is also a good option, since it's nutritious, filling, and higher in fiber.

**CORN:** Another essential grain in African cuisines. We use corn in many forms: fresh, dried, and ground into cornmeal or flour.

**LEGUMES:** Lentils and beans are also very popular in African cuisines, since they're delicious and easy to store. Black-eyed peas, with their funny black-and-white coloring, are my favorite.

**GRAINS:** African cuisines feature many lesser-known grains, such as fonio, teff, sorghum, and millet (all gluten-free and incredibly rich in nutrients).

## Fats

We shouldn't eliminate fats from our diet. Eaten in moderation, they provide us with beneficial fatty acids and help our nervous systems to function properly. But note that different oils have different uses in the kitchen. My favorite oils for cooking are virgin coconut oil and peanut oil.

For seasoning or salad dressings, I like to use cold-pressed virgin olive oil, sesame oil, and walnut oil. I also use peanut butter, coconut cream, and sesame paste (tahini) to add unique flavors to my dishes.

## Preserves/Canned Goods

Of course, I favor fresh fruits and veggies whenever possible. It's also practical to have some canned goods in your pantry. I always like to have a few on hand; my favorites are chickpeas and kidney beans. I also recommend keeping canned tomato products—crushed tomatoes, tomato sauce, tomato paste, sun-dried tomatoes—on hand. You can buy tomatoes in the summertime and preserve them to use all year long.

*Spices*

When you think of African cuisines, you may think of spices. Spices and aromatic herbs are a must! We use them in main dishes, desserts, and even drinks! Truly magical ingredients, spices can awaken and transform any dish.

Season your African-inspired dishes with ginger, Penja white pepper from Cameroon (the best in the world in my opinion), garlic, nutmeg, cinnamon, vanilla from Madagascar, cumin, preserved lemon, tamarind, apki (seeds from the djansang fruit tree that are widely used in Ivorian and Cameroonian cuisine), soumbala (also called soumbara, netetou in Wolof, dawadawa in Igbo, ôdji in Poular, irù in Yoruba, and afitin in Fon-Gbe), a fragrant, caroblike condiment made from the seeds of the néré tree, used in West African cuisines), and raw or roasted cacao beans. Don't forget that herbs, fresh or dried, are a true delicacy!

And, of course, there's the famous chile pepper! Chile peppers are beloved for their enchanting scent and inimitable flavor. They are widely used, in all their colors and forms, across the African continent. Even so, they aren't used in every African dish. In fact, it's important to remember that "spiced" doesn't always mean "spicy." It's all about the amount. If you don't like spicy food, don't panic: The recipes in this book are suitable for even the most sensitive of palates.

## AFRICAN SUPERFOODS

I love these feel-good foods, both for their flavor and their health benefits.

**AVOCADO:** Don't avoid avocados just because they're high in fat. These fruits are rich in beneficial fatty acids that can lower cholesterol, which means they're great for cardiovascular health. Avocados also contain vitamins A, B6, C, and E, as well as iron, magnesium, phosphorus, and zinc.

**CACAO:** Raw cacao is rich in magnesium and theobromine. It's a natural antidepressant and helps the body fight stress and fatigue. Raw cacao plants also contain flavonoids, antioxidant compounds that slow cellular aging.

**GARLIC:** Though sometimes avoided because of its strong odor, garlic is appreciated in so many African cuisines that it would be a shame to avoid it. When eaten raw, it contains antibiotic and antimicrobial properties. Garlic also helps to prevents cardiovascular disease by regulating cholesterol and helps to prevent cancers by boosting the immune system.

**GINGER:** When eaten regularly, ginger has positive effects on digestion while also stimulating the immune system. A natural tonic, it's also considered an aphrodisiac.

**KINKELIBA:** A bushy shrub generally found on the plains of West Africa, kinkeliba is traditionally infused into teas, which allows you to reap the benefits of its diuretic properties. It relieves digestive problems, stimulates biliary function, and helps to protect liver cells. It's also anti-inflammatory and antibacterial.

**SWEET POTATO:** Rich in vitamins A, B2, B5, B6, C, copper, magnesium, and potassium, the sweet potato is an ingredient as delicious as it is healthy. It's full of antioxidants and great for skin health. It also protects against hypertension and cardiovascular disease.

# SAUCES

---

# IVORIAN VINAIGRETTE
## Virgin Sauce

MAKES ABOUT 2½ CUPS (900 G)
**PREP TIME:** 15 minutes

*This vinaigrette is a blend of raw veggies that traditionally accompany attiéké (cassava couscous; see page 64) in Ivorian cuisine. It also pairs well with Alloco (Fried Plantains, page 32) or Sweet Potato Fries (page 36). Each cook has their own version of this vinaigrette; it can be made with or without cucumbers or chile peppers, with thinly sliced or minced vegetables . . . the possibilities are endless! But there's one important ingredient in every version: raw onion. It will keep in the refrigerator for 24 hours.*

3 tablespoons white balsamic vinegar

1 tablespoon Dijon mustard

1 tablespoon olive oil

1 vegetable stock cube, crumbled

2 tomatoes, diced

1 cucumber, diced

1 yellow onion, thinly sliced

1 green chile pepper (such as jalapeño), diced, optional

2 garlic cloves, thinly sliced

Black pepper

1. Whisk the vinegar, mustard, and oil together in a small bowl. Add the stock cube and whisk until smooth.

2. Add the tomatoes, cucumber, onion, chile (if using), and garlic, season with pepper, and whisk again.

# TOMATO SAUCE

MAKES ABOUT 2 CUPS (800 G)

PREP TIME: 15 minutes ✦ COOK TIME: 30 minutes

*In Côte d'Ivoire, there are as many tomato sauce recipes as there are families. This one is inspired by my mother's famous recipe. It can be paired with a variety of foods, including Alloco (Fried Plantains, page 32), attiéké (cassava couscous; see page 64), yam, sweet potato, or white rice.*

5 tomatoes, diced

2 large onions, diced

1 habanero chile pepper or mini red bell pepper, diced

4 garlic cloves

¼ cup (60 ml) olive oil

1 teaspoon tomato paste

1 vegetable stock cube, crumbled

Black pepper

1. Mix the tomatoes, onions, habanero, and garlic together in a large bowl until well combined.

2. Heat the oil in a large pot over medium heat, add the tomato paste, and stir until slightly darkened in color, 1 minute.

3. Add the vegetables and the stock cube. Season with black pepper and stir for about 1 minute. Bring to a simmer and cook until thickened, stirring occasionally, for 30 minutes.

# SATINI COTOMILI
## Cilantro Chutney

MAKES ABOUT 1½ CUPS (400 G)

PREP TIME: 10 minutes

*Satini cotomili is a Creole recipe that comes from the island of Mauritius. The sauce is an essential condiment in Mauritian cuisine, where it is served with roasted or grilled vegetables, beignets (see Plantain Beignets, page 28), and crêpes (see Savory Mauritian Crêpes, page 45). It will keep in the refrigerator for 24 hours.*

2 tomatoes, diced

1 white onion, chopped

1 bunch cilantro

1 green chile pepper (such as jalapeño), halved, seeds removed if desired

1 large garlic clove, halved

2 tablespoons white vinegar

Salt

Black pepper

Place the tomatoes, onion, cilantro, chile, garlic, white vinegar, and ½ cup (120 ml) water in a food processor. Season with salt and pepper, then process until smooth.

# MANGO-CHILE SAUCE

MAKES ABOUT 3 CUPS (800 G)

PREP TIME: 15 minutes ◆ COOK TIME: 25 minutes

*I love the taste of chile peppers, and I add them to many of my dishes. Even so, I'm not a big fan of spicy food. I prefer the subtle presence of a mild chile pepper, which adds heat that doesn't overwhelm, like in this mango-chile sauce. It's a perfect companion to grilled or roasted vegetables, beignets (see Plantain Beignets, page 28), or even burgers (see Yassa Burger, page 108). It will keep for 1 week in the refrigerator.*

3 ripe mangoes, peeled and chopped

1 yellow onion, thinly sliced

1 yellow bell pepper, diced

1 Scotch bonnet pepper, diced

2 tablespoons olive oil

1 teaspoon minced fresh ginger

1 tablespoon curry powder

1 teaspoon paprika

1 teaspoon sugar

1 teaspoon ground turmeric

Salt

Black pepper

Juice of ½ orange

1 tablespoon apple cider vinegar

1. Mix the mangoes, onion, yellow pepper, and Scotch bonnet pepper in a medium bowl.

2. Heat the oil in a pan over low heat. Add the mango-onion-pepper mixture and the ginger. Cook until softened, stirring frequently, about 5 minutes.

3. Add the curry powder, paprika, sugar, turmeric, pinch of salt and black pepper, and stir. Add the orange juice and vinegar, then simmer on low until thickened, 20 minutes. Let cool.

# NOKOSS VERT
## Senegalese Green Pepper Paste

MAKES ABOUT 1½ CUPS (400 G)

**PREP TIME:** 15 minutes

*Nokoss is a sauce from Senegal, but similar sauces exist across many African cultures.
It's so flavorful! I use this sauce as a marinade or serve it alongside roasted or grilled vegetables.
It will keep for 24 hours in the refrigerator.*

1 green bell pepper, diced

4 scallions, minced

1 green chile pepper (such as jalapeño), diced

6 garlic cloves, chopped

One ¼-inch (6 mm) piece of ginger, chopped

1 bunch parsley

10 mint leaves

2 tablespoons olive oil

1 vegetable stock cube, crumbled

Black pepper

1. Place the bell pepper, scallions, chile, garlic, and ginger in a food processor and process for 30 seconds.

2. Add the parsley, mint, oil, and stock cube. Season with pepper and process again to form a smooth paste, about 1 minute. Add more oil if needed to achieve your desired consistency.

# PERI-PERI SAUCE

MAKES ABOUT 1½ CUPS (350 G)

PREP TIME: 10 minutes  ✦  COOK TIME: 20 minutes

*This spicy sauce can elevate any dish. Don't hesitate to modify the number of peppers according to your spice tolerance and preference.*

3 tomatoes, seeds removed and roughly chopped

10 peri-peri peppers or habanero chile pepper, seeds removed and roughly chopped

1 red onion, sliced

4 garlic cloves, sliced

2 tablespoons chopped parsley

1 vegetable stock cube, crumbled

⅔ cup (160 ml) vegetable oil

Salt

1. Place the tomatoes, peppers, onion, garlic, parsley, and stock cube in a food processor. Add the oil and process until smooth.

2. Transfer the mixture to a saucepan, stir, and bring to a boil. Lower the heat and simmer until thickened, 20 minutes, stirring frequently to prevent the sauce from sticking to the pan. Season with salt to taste. Let cool.

3. Store in an airtight container, covered with oil, in the refrigerator for up to 1 week.

# SNACKS

---

# CRUNCHY SPICED CHICKPEAS

SERVES 4

**PREP TIME:** 5 minutes ✦ **COOK TIME:** 20 minutes

*This crunchy chickpea recipe is inspired by my trips to Morocco, where chickpeas are a staple. You can use any spice you'd like for this recipe: cumin, ras el hanout, paprika, curry powder. Don't be afraid to experiment! Eat these delicious chickpeas as a snack or use them as a topping for a salad or a power bowl (see Gratitude Bowl, page 114). Be creative!*

One 15-ounce (425 g) can of chickpeas, rinsed and patted dry

2 tablespoons olive oil

1 tablespoon curry powder

1 tablespoon paprika

Pinch of salt

Pinch of sugar

1. Preheat the oven to 350°F (180°C). Line a baking sheet with foil.

2. Mix the chickpeas, oil, curry powder, paprika, salt, and sugar together in a bowl. Transfer them to the baking sheet and bake for 20 minutes, until crispy and golden brown.

# ROASTED SWEET POTATO HUMMUS

MAKES ABOUT 2 CUPS (500 G)

**PREP TIME:** 10 minutes ✦ **COOK TIME:** 30 minutes

*This recipe, like the Crunchy Spiced Chickpeas (page 18), is a mix of flavors from North and sub-Saharan Africa. I never tire of offering this dish to my guests. It's always a hit!*

1 medium sweet potato, peeled and diced

2 tablespoons olive oil, plus more for drizzling

Half a 15-ounce (425g) can chickpeas

½ cup chickpea liquid from the can

2 tablespoons tahini

Juice of 1 lime

1 teaspoon garlic powder

Pinch of smoked paprika

Salt

Black pepper

1. Preheat the oven to 350°F (180°C). Line a baking sheet with parchment paper.

2. Place the potato on the baking sheet. Season with oil, salt, and pepper and bake for 30 minutes, until cooked through and starting to brown. Transfer to a blender.

3. Drain and rinse the chickpeas, setting aside the reserved ½ cup (120 ml) chickpea liquid from the can. Add the chickpeas, tahini, lime juice, garlic powder, and paprika to the blender. Blend until smooth. Slowly add the chickpea liquid to achieve your desired consistency.

4. Add more salt, pepper, and oil, if desired, before serving.

# PEANUT HUMMUS

MAKES ABOUT 2 CUPS (500 G)

**PREP TIME:** 10 minutes ✦ **COOK TIME:** 5 minutes

*This quick and tasty recipe is a great snack to serve to guests. You can also add this hummus to a bowl, sandwich, or salad.*

One 15-ounce (425 g) can chickpeas

½ cup chickpea liquid from the can

2 tablespoons peanut butter

Juice of 1 lime

1 teaspoon garlic powder

Pinch of paprika

½ cup (75 g) peanuts

1 tablespoon olive oil

Salt

Black pepper

1. Drain and rinse the chickpeas, setting aside the reserved ½ cup (120 ml) chickpea liquid from the can. Place the chickpeas, peanut butter, lime juice, garlic powder, and paprika in a blender and blend until smooth.

2. Slowly add the chickpea liquid to taste to achieve your desired consistency.

3. Heat a heavy frying pan over high heat and toast the peanuts for about 5 minutes. Add them to the chickpea mixture and stir gently.

4. Season with salt and pepper to taste and drizzle with oil before serving.

# SWEET PEPPER AND CORN CAKES

### MAKES 4 CAKES

**PREP TIME:** 15 minutes ✦ **COOK TIME:** 4 minutes

*Cakes like these are very common in many African cuisines, often eaten as street food. Inexpensive and filling, they're eaten on the go with chutneys or sauces. They are a perfect companion to soups or sautéed vegetables. They also make a great appetizer.*

⅓ cup (50g) fine cornmeal

⅓ cup (50g) whole wheat flour

1 teaspoon garlic powder

1 teaspoon paprika

½ teaspoon baking powder

2 parsley sprigs, minced

One 15-ounce (425g) can corn, drained

3 tablespoons almond milk

Salt

Black pepper

½ red bell pepper, diced

1 tablespoon vegetable oil

1. Mix the cornmeal, flour, garlic powder, paprika, baking powder, and parsley together in a medium bowl.

2. Mix about three quarters of the corn and the almond milk together in a second bowl. Season with salt and pepper and add this to the dry ingredients in the first bowl.

3. Gently stir the remaining corn and the bell pepper into the corn mixture. Stir well to combine. Form the mixture into 4 equal patties.

4. Heat the oil in a large frying pan over medium heat. Add the patties, flatten them slightly, and cook until golden brown, 2 minutes on each side. Drain them on paper or kitchen towels before serving.

# RED BEAN CAKES

MAKES 4 CAKES

**PREP TIME:** 10 minutes ✦ **COOK TIME:** 8 minutes

*These Red Bean Cakes make delicious burgers. In addition to being high in protein, they're also full of flavor and incredibly versatile. You can shape them in so many ways: as steaks, dumplings, or even quenelles.*

One 15.5-ounce (439 g) red kidney beans, drained and rinsed

⅓ cup (35 g) bread crumbs

3 tablespoons cornstarch

1 shallot, minced

1 teaspoon garlic powder

1 teaspoon mustard

1 teaspoon minced parsley

Pinch of ground cumin

Pinch of smoked paprika

Salt

Black pepper

¼ cup (60 ml) olive oil

1. Coarsely mash the beans in a large bowl. Add 2 tablespoons water and mix.

2. Add the bread crumbs, cornstarch, shallot, garlic powder, mustard, parsley, cumin, and paprika. Add salt and pepper to taste. Form the mixture into 4 equal patties.

3. Heat the oil in a large frying pan over medium heat. Place the patties in the pan and cook until golden brown, 4 minutes on each side.

# SWEET POTATO AND GINGER LOAF

MAKES ONE 9 × 5-INCH (23 × 13 CM) LOAF, 4 SERVINGS

**PREP TIME:** 15 minutes ✦ **COOK TIME:** 1 hour, 25 minutes

*This sweet potato loaf can be enjoyed on any occasion: as an appetizer with a chutney or sauce, as a snack, or even as a dessert with jam or a scoop of ice cream.*

3 medium sweet potatoes (about 21 ounces/600 g), diced

1 cup (140 g) rice flour, plus more for dusting

⅔ cup (160 ml) hazelnut or almond milk

⅓ cup (40 g) almond meal

⅓ cup (60 g) coconut sugar (or brown sugar)

1 tablespoon lemon juice

1 teaspoon baking powder

1 teaspoon grated ginger (or ground ginger)

½ teaspoon coconut oil, plus more for oiling

½ teaspoon ground nutmeg

Pinch of salt

1. Preheat the oven to 350°F (180°C). Line a baking sheet with parchment paper.

2. Bake the sweet potatoes for about 35 minutes, until golden brown and caramelized. Set them aside to cool.

3. Transfer the cooled sweet potatoes to a large bowl and mash. Add the rice flour, hazelnut milk, almond meal, sugar, lemon juice, baking powder, ginger, coconut oil, and nutmeg, and mix thoroughly.

4. Oil a 9 x 5-inch (23 x 13 cm) loaf pan and dust with flour. Transfer the batter to the pan.

5. Bake for 50 minutes, until a tester inserted into the center comes out clean. Let cool, then remove from the pan and slice.

# PLANTAIN BEIGNETS

### SERVES 4

**PREP TIME:** 10 minutes ✦ **COOK TIME:** 4 minutes per beignet ✦ **REST TIME:** 20 minutes

*Also known as claclo or clacro in Côte d'Ivoire, these Plantain Beignets were initially just a way to use too-ripe plantains before they spoiled. Along with spices, a little bit of flour and vegetable oil is all you need to transform plantains destined for the trash can into gold. My sister, who adores these lovely little beignets, sometimes adds a handful of cooked rice to the dough. The result: spongy beignets with a bit of crunch.*

4 ripe plantains, peeled and sliced

3 tablespoons all-purpose flour

1 shallot, minced

1 garlic clove, minced

1 teaspoon grated ginger (optional)

Pinch of cayenne

Salt

Black pepper

Canola oil, for frying

1. Mash the plantains in a mortar or bowl, then add the flour. Add the shallot, garlic, ginger, cayenne, salt, and pepper, and mix well. Set aside for about 20 minutes.

2. Heat a layer of oil in a large skillet over medium-high heat. Drop small spoonfuls of the dough into the hot oil and cook until golden brown, about 4 minutes. Continue cooking the rest of the dough until all the beignets are cooked.

# SPICED POPCORN

**PREP TIME:** 2 minutes ✦ **COOK TIME:** 5 minutes

*Sometimes I joke that popcorn is my favorite meal, so it's only fair that this recipe found its way into this book. In Côte d'Ivoire, where it is sold by street vendors in paper cones or small plastic bags, we call it bon maïs, which means "good corn." It's not necessarily eaten at the movies as is often the case in the West; we enjoy this popcorn at any time of day. It's also sometimes given to guests at parties.*

1½ cups (200 g) popcorn kernels

3 tablespoons peanut or sunflower oil

1 tablespoon ras el hanout

Salt

1. Mix the popcorn and oil together in a small bowl. Transfer to a pot, cover, and cook over medium heat.

2. When the popcorn begin to pop, move the pot around without uncovering it. After about 3 minutes, or when the popping has stopped, turn off the heat.

3. Sprinkle with ras el hanout and salt, and enjoy while hot.

---

NOTE: *You can also make sweet Spiced Popcorn, with cinnamon and coconut sugar. Use any spices you like. The possibilities are endless.*

---

# ALLOCO
## Fried Plantains

SERVES 4

**PREP TIME:** 5 minutes  ✦  **COOK TIME:** 5 minutes

*Though it's difficult to pin down the origin of this recipe, it's adored in sub-Saharan Africa. Fried, boiled, or mashed, sweet or savory, plantains are an essential staple ingredient in many African cuisines. The name "alloco" is Ivorian, but this dish has a host of other names: makemba in the Democratic Republic of Congo, amanda in Togo, and dodo in Nigeria. Alloco has an addictive quality for some, who can't go a full day without a plate of it. Pair with a spicy tomato sauce.*

4 ripe plantains, peeled and
   sliced ¼ inch (2 cm) thick
Salt
Canola oil, for frying

1. Place the plantain slices in a bowl, season with salt, and mix gently.

2. Heat the oil in a large pot over high heat. Fry until golden-brown, about 5 minutes.

3. Transfer to paper or kitchen towels to drain. Season with salt to taste and enjoy immediately.

# PAPRIKA-SPICED PLANTAIN CHIPS

### SERVES 4

**PREP TIME:** 10 minutes ✦ **COOK TIME:** 20 minutes

*The unripe plantains used in this recipe, though technically fruits, are eaten like vegetables. They contain concentrated starches and must be cooked before eating. Though this recipe uses an oven, in West Africa, it's not uncommon to see women preparing these chips on the side of the road in large pots of hot oil.*

Vegetable oil cooking spray

2 green plantains, peeled and very thinly sliced

1 teaspoon paprika

Salt

Black pepper

1. Preheat the oven to 400°F (200°C). Spray a baking sheet with cooking spray.

2. Place the plantain slices on the baking sheet in a single layer without touching. Spray again with cooking spray, and sprinkle with paprika, salt, and pepper.

3. Cook for about 10 minutes, then flip them and cook for 10 minutes, until golden brown. Enjoy warm or at room temperature.

TIP: *For a quicker cook time, you can fry the plantain slices in a pot of hot oil for a few minutes.*

# SWEET POTATO FRIES

**PREP TIME:** 5 minutes ✦ **COOK TIME:** 40 minutes

*In my mother's village, close to Bouaflé in Côte d'Ivoire, they make this recipe with pinkish-white sweet potatoes, which are locally grown. They're cut into thick fries, cooked in a fryer, then lightly salted—that's all! So simple and delightful, this dish from my childhood inspired me to develop this recipe for crunchy, spiced fries.*

2 medium sweet potatoes (about 14 ounces/400 g), cut into matchsticks

2 tablespoons coconut oil

2 tablespoons nutritional yeast

1 teaspoon garlic powder

1 teaspoon smoked paprika

Salt

1. Preheat the oven to 350°F (180°C). Line a baking sheet with parchment paper.

2. Place the sweet potato matchsticks in a large bowl, then add the oil, yeast, garlic powder, and paprika. Shake the bowl to evenly distribute the ingredients.

3. Place the fries on the baking sheet and bake for 30 to 40 minutes, until golden brown and crispy. Sprinkle with salt and serve.

# CHAPATI
## East African Flatbread

MAKES 8 CHAPATI

**PREP TIME:** 20 minutes ✦ **COOK TIME:** 30 minutes ✦ **REST TIME:** 30 minutes

*Chapati is an unleavened bread of Indian origin. It is eaten in many African countries, such as Burundi, Uganda, Mozambique, and Kenya, and can be paired with almost any dish, savory or sweet.*

2¾ cups (375 g) all-purpose flour, plus more for kneading

1 teaspoon salt

3 tablespoons vegetable oil, plus more for brushing

1¼ cup (300 ml) warm water

1. Gently mix the flour, salt, and oil together in a large bowl. Gradually add the water and mix to form a sticky, soft dough.

2. Transfer the dough to a clean, floured work surface. Knead until the dough becomes smooth and elastic, 10 to 15 minutes. Return the dough to the bowl, cover with plastic wrap, and let sit in a warm place for 20 to 30 minutes.

3. Transfer the dough to a floured surface and divide it into 8 equal parts. Roll into balls with your hands, then roll each ball with a rolling pin into a very thin, round chapati.

4. Heat a nonstick or heavy-bottomed frying pan over high heat. Place one chapati in the pan and let it cook, undisturbed, for a few seconds. Brush the top with a thin layer of oil. When bubbles appear on the surface, flip and brush the other side with a thin layer of oil.

5. Flip one or two more times until each side is golden brown to your liking.

6. Continue cooking the rest of the chapatis until they are all cooked. Serve warm.

# SWEET BREAD

MAKES 10 ROLLS

**PREP TIME:** 20 minutes ✦ **COOK TIME:** 15 minutes ✦ **REST TIME:** 6½ hours

*Sweet Bread, or "pain sucré," is a spongy bread that was brought to Côte d'Ivoire by Ghanaian immigrants. It's also commonly associated with Bassam, the site of the country's colonial capital. Bassam is home to many groups of Akan people, including my father's, the Nzima. The Akan people are mostly distributed between Ghana and Côte d'Ivoire, and for hundreds of years, their culinary borders have been fluid. Today, these sweet rolls are an integral part of Ivorian street food, eaten at all times of day. I love to eat them, as is or toasted, with breakfast or as a snack. They're also great for sandwiches.*

½ cup (120 ml) warm water

1 teaspoon active dry yeast

1¾ cups (250 g) all-purpose flour

⅓ cup (60 g) sugar

1 vanilla bean, scraped

1½ teaspoons salt

3 tablespoons vegetable oil

1. Mix the warm water and yeast together in a small bowl. Let proof for 5 minutes.

2. Mix the flour, sugar, and vanilla together in a medium bowl or a stand mixer. Add the yeast mixture.

3. Knead the dough for about 5 minutes, then add the salt. Incorporate the oil slowly, one tablespoon at a time. Continue kneading until the dough is smooth and elastic, about 10 minutes.

4. Form the dough into a ball and place in a large bowl. Cover with plastic wrap and let rise for 2 hours, until doubled in size.

5. Flour a work surface, roll out the dough, and reform it into a large ball. Wrap with plastic wrap and let sit in the refrigerator for 3 hours.

6. Divide the dough into 10 equal pieces. Form each piece into a compact ball, then place on a baking sheet. Cover with plastic wrap and let sit for 1 hour, 30 minutes.

7. Preheat the oven to 350°F (180°C) and bake the rolls for 15 minutes, until golden brown.

# INJERA
## Ethiopian Flatbread

MAKES 4 FLATBREADS

**PREP TIME:** 10 minutes ✦ **COOK TIME:** 20 minutes ✦ **REST TIME:** 24 hours

*Injera is a traditional sour flatbread eaten in many African countries, most notably Ethiopia and Eritrea. It is typically placed on a large plate and then covered with various sauces or spreads. It can also be pulled apart and used to scoop up stews and salads.*

4 cups (960 ml) warm water
1 teaspoon active dry yeast
5 cups (600 g) fine millet flour
Pinch of baking soda

1. Mix ¼ cup (60 ml) water and the yeast together in a large bowl and let sit for 5 minutes. Add the remaining ¾ cup water, add the flour, and mix well.

2. Cover the bowl with a clean, dry cloth and let rise for 24 hours at room temperature.

3. Add the baking soda and mix again.

4. Heat a nonstick or heavy-bottomed frying pan over medium heat and add a ladleful of batter to the pan. Gently tilt the pan to spread the batter across the entire surface.

5. Cover the pan and let cook until bubbles appear on the surface of the batter, about 1 minute.

6. Slide the flatbread onto a plate and continue to cook the remaining batter to make three more injera.

# COCO BREAD

MAKES 4 ROLLS

**PREP TIME:** 15 minutes  ✦  **COOK TIME:** 30 minutes  ✦  **REST TIME:** 30 minutes

*Now that I've confessed my love for Sweet Bread (page 41), I'll tell you something else: I often find myself falling for Sweet Bread's cousin, Coco Bread. I love coco bread's sweet coconut aroma, its golden-brown color, and its comforting flavor. It can be eaten as is or used to make French toast. If you love sweet and salty flavors, use Coco Bread to make sandwiches.*

One ¼-ounce (7 g) packet active dry yeast

1 cup (240 ml) coconut milk, warmed

¼ cup (60 ml) coconut oil, plus more for oiling

2 tablespoons coconut sugar

2 tablespoons granulated sugar

1 teaspoon salt

3½ cups (480 g) all-purpose flour, plus more for kneading

½ cup (50 g) unsweetened shredded coconut

1 teaspoon ground nutmeg

1. Oil a baking sheet.

2. Mix the yeast and coconut milk in a large bowl. Let rest for about 1 minute.

3. Add the oil, coconut sugar, granulated sugar, and salt. Mix well to dissolve the sugar, then add the flour, coconut, and nutmeg. Use your fingers to mix the ingredients together to form a sticky dough.

4. Place the dough on a clean floured work surface and knead to form a smooth dough, about 5 minutes.

5. Return the dough to the bowl, cover with plastic wrap, and let rise for 20 minutes.

6. Divide the dough into 4 equal parts and roll each one into 2-inch-thick (5 cm) buns.

7. Score the buns with a fork and let rest for 10 minutes. Preheat the oven to 375°F (190°C).

8. Place the buns on the baking sheet and bake them for about 25 minutes, until golden brown.

# SAVORY
# MAURITIAN CRÊPES

MAKES 5 CRÊPES

**PREP TIME:** 10 minutes ✦ **COOK TIME:** 10 minutes ✦ **REST TIME:** 1 hour

*Savory crêpes are both disarmingly simple and disarmingly delicious. This is a traditional Indo-Mauritian recipe. For many Mauritians, these crêpes are comfort food, even eaten during cyclones. Enjoy your crêpes just like they do on the island of Mauritius, fresh from the pan, served with Satini Cotomili (Cilantro Chutney, page 11).*

1⅓ cups (200 g) whole wheat
  flour

1 teaspoon salt

½ teaspoon ground turmeric

2 tablespoons minced chives

1 tablespoon vegetable oil,
  plus more for frying

1⅔ cups (400 ml) warm water

1. Combine the flour, salt, turmeric, chives, and oil in a large bowl. Slowly add the water, whisking constantly to remove any lumps and form a smooth batter.

2. Place the bowl in the refrigerator for 1 hour to thicken the batter.

3. Heat a layer of oil in a nonstick frying pan over medium heat. Add a ladleful of batter to the pan and gently tilt the pan so the batter covers the entire surface. Cook until the bottom is golden brown, about 1 minute. Loosen the edges with a spatula, flip the crêpe over, and cook on the other side, about 1 minute. Slide the crêpe off the pan and onto a plate. Cover with foil to keep warm.

4. Repeat with the remaining batter. Enjoy immediately.

# STARTERS

—

# ROASTED EGGPLANT WITH TAMARIND

### SERVES 4

**PREP TIME:** 15 minutes  ◆  **SOAK TIME:** 20 minutes  ◆  **COOK TIME:** 45 minutes

*Roasted eggplant is typically found in thieboudienne (tiep), the national dish of Senegal. It inspired me to create this recipe for deliciously soft eggplants. Serve it as a starter or with rice or couscous.*

¼ cup (50 g) tamarind paste

⅔ cup (160 ml) warm water

2 large eggplants

½ cup (120 ml) olive oil

¼ cup (45 g) coconut sugar

1 teaspoon soy sauce

Salt

Black pepper

1. Preheat the oven to 425°F (220°C).

2. Soak the tamarind paste in warm water for 20 minutes, then mix well to dissolve it entirely. Strain through a fine mesh strainer, reserving the tamarind liquid.

3. Halve the eggplants lengthwise, then score the flesh in a crosshatch pattern, without cutting through the skin. Slather in oil and generously season with salt and pepper. Place the eggplants on a baking sheet and roast for 30 minutes.

4. While the eggplants cook, place the tamarind liquid, sugar, and soy sauce in a small saucepan and mix well. Bring to a boil, stirring occasionally, reduce the heat to low, and simmer until thickened, 5 minutes.

5. Remove the eggplants from the oven, coat with the sauce, and return them to the oven for 15 minutes, until the eggplants are golden and tender.

TIP: *Place a heat-resistant container filled with water at the bottom of the oven to prevent the eggplants from drying out and cracking.*

# SWEET POTATO SALAD WITH MIXED BABY GREENS AND CASHEWS

### SERVES 4

**PREP TIME:** 10 minutes  ✦  **COOK TIME:** 35 minutes

*I originally developed this recipe to use leftover roasted sweet potatoes, along with whatever I had in the fridge at the time. This salad is easy to customize, so don't hesitate to do so. Try replacing the cashews with roasted peanuts or the mixed shoots with mesclun greens or fresh baby spinach leaves.*

2 tablespoons sesame oil

2 teaspoons garlic powder

1 teaspoon paprika

1 teaspoon herbes de Provence

Salt

Black pepper

2 medium sweet potatoes, diced

½ cup (65 g) cashews

½ red onion

Juice of 1 lemon

1 tablespoon pomegranate molasses

1 handful of mixed baby greens

1. Preheat the oven to 350°F (180°C). Line a baking sheet with parchment paper.

2. Mix 1 tablespoon of the oil, 1 teaspoon of the garlic powder, the paprika, herbes de Provence, salt, and pepper in a large bowl. Add the sweet potatoes and toss well to coat.

3. Transfer the potato mixture to the baking sheet and bake for about 35 minutes, until golden brown. Let cool.

4. While the potatoes are cooking, heat a dry skillet over medium-high heat and lightly toast the cashews, 5 minutes. Set aside.

5. Mix together the onion, lemon juice, pomegranate molasses, the remaining 1 tablespoon sesame oil, and the remaining 1 teaspoon garlic powder in a small bowl to make a vinaigrette. Add salt and pepper to taste.

6. Place the greens in a large bowl, then add the vinaigrette and toss.

7. To serve, place the greens on a plate, add the roasted potatoes and top with the cashews.

# RED CABBAGE SALAD WITH MANGO AND PEANUTS

SERVES 4

**PREP TIME:** 15 minutes ✦ **COOK TIME:** 1 minute

*In West Africa, it's common to start a meal with a large salad full of different types of raw vegetables, especially at family gatherings. In the blink of an eye, this red cabbage salad will become a must-have. And while you might be tempted to avoid salads to save room for the delicious main courses that are sure to follow, I bet you can't resist this one!*

1 small red cabbage, outer leaves removed, halved, and thinly sliced

1 ripe but firm mango, peeled and thinly sliced

1 bunch cilantro, chopped

1 bunch mint, leaves chopped

1 green chile pepper (such as jalapeño), chopped

1 scallion, chopped

Juice of 1 lemon

2 tablespoons sesame oil

1 teaspoon garlic powder

½ cup (75 g) peanuts

Salt

Black pepper

1. Bring a large pot of water to a boil. Fill a bowl with ice water. Blanch the cabbage in the pot for about 1 minute, then transfer immediately to the bowl of ice water to stop further cooking. Drain the cooled cabbage on paper or kitchen towels. Transfer the cabbage to a large bowl.

2. Add the mango, cilantro, mint, chile, and scallion to the bowl.

3. To make the dressing, mix the lemon juice, sesame oil, garlic powder, salt, and black pepper together in a small bowl.

4. Pour the dressing over the red cabbage and toss to combine the flavors. Top with peanuts. Serve immediately or place in the refrigerator for 1 hour before serving.

# MANGO, AVOCADO, AND RADISH SALAD

SERVES 4

**PREP TIME:** 15 minutes

*I remember watching my grandmother Bintou eat ripe mangos so small that she could fit them in her mouth whole. Mango was her favorite fruit, so I developed this recipe for her. It's a super-fresh salad with a dressing of lemon juice and sesame oil, but you can also eat it with peanut-ginger sauce (see Roasted Cauliflower with Peanut-Ginger Sauce, page 62).*

1 ripe but firm mango, peeled and chopped

1 avocado, peeled and chopped

1 bunch radishes, tops removed, thinly sliced

1 bunch mint, leaves chopped

Juice of 1 lemon

1 tablespoon sesame oil

Salt

Black pepper

1. Place the mango, avocado, radishes, and mint leaves in a large bowl.

2. Sprinkle in the lemon juice, then add the sesame oil, salt, and pepper. Mix gently to avoid crushing the avocado.

3. Serve immediately.

# CUMIN-SPICED ORANGE
# AND CHICKPEA SALAD

SERVES 4

**PREP TIME:** 15 minutes

*Orange salad is a Moroccan dessert I love. Fresh and subtly flavored with orange blossom water or cinnamon, I often serve this dish to guests in the summer. This recipe is a savory version, with similar lightness and flavor.*

3 oranges, peeled and sectioned

Half a 15-ounce (425 g) can chickpeas, rinsed and patted dry

1 red onion, thinly sliced

3 flat-leaf parsley sprigs, chopped

Juice of 1 lemon

2 tablespoons olive oil

1 teaspoon ground cumin

1 teaspoon paprika

Salt

Black pepper

1. Combine the orange sections, chickpeas, onion, and parsley in a large bowl.

2. To make the dressing, mix the lemon juice, oil, cumin, paprika, salt, and pepper in a small bowl. Add the dressing to the salad and toss. Serve on the side.

# KACHUMBARI
## East African Tomato and Onion Salad

SERVES 4

**PREP TIME:** 10 minutes

*Kachumbari is a Swahili salad that is very popular in East Africa, especially Kenya, Burundi, and Tanzania. In Malawi, it's called chum. In India, similar preparations are known as kachumber.*

4 tomatoes, chopped

1 red bell pepper, chopped

1 cucumber, chopped

1 red onion, thinly sliced

2 garlic cloves, thinly sliced

½ bunch cilantro or parsley, leaves chopped

Juice of 2 lemons

1 tablespoon olive oil

Salt

Black pepper

1. Combine the tomatoes, bell pepper, cucumber, onion, garlic, and cilantro in a large bowl.

2. Sprinkle with lemon juice and oil. Season with salt and black pepper and toss to combine.

3. Serve immediately.

# FONIO AND PAPAYA SALAD

SERVES 4

PREP TIME: 15 minutes ✦ COOK TIME: 5 minutes

*This salad features a delicious, much-loved West African grain that's still underappreciated in the West: fonio. In addition to being gluten-free, it's also packed with the B vitamins (thiamine, riboflavin, and niacin) and minerals, including iron, copper, and magnesium. It's also a good source of fiber and plant protein. I often eat steaming-hot fonio in place of rice.*

1 cup (200 g) fonio, rinsed

Juice of 1 lemon

Pinch of ground cumin

2 tablespoons olive oil

Salt

Black pepper

2 tomatoes, diced

1 firm papaya, peeled and diced

½ red onion, minced

½ cup (65 g) roasted cashews

1 cup (50 g) chopped mint leaves

½ bunch flat-leaf parsley, chopped

1. Place the fonio in a small saucepan with 2 cups (480 ml) water. Bring to a boil. Add a pinch of salt, stir, cover, and reduce the heat to low for 1 minute. Turn off the heat and let sit, covered, for 5 minutes. Fluff with a fork, then transfer to a large bowl to cool.

2. Mix the lemon juice, cumin, salt, and pepper in a small bowl. Slowly add the olive oil, whisking to emulsify.

3. Add the tomatoes, papaya, onion, cashews, mint, and parsley to the fonio. Drizzle with the dressing, toss to mix, and serve.

TIP: *For an even more refreshing salad, place in the refrigerator for 30 minutes before serving.*

# RED CABBAGE SALAD WITH MANGO AND RAW OKRA

SERVES 4

**PREP TIME:** 15 minutes ◆ **COOK TIME:** 1 minute

*Okra is a popular vegetable in West African cuisines. It is rich in vitamin C and antioxidants and can be eaten in so many ways: in soups, stews, sauces, and more. This recipe uses okra in a less-common form— raw—to allow the flavor to really shine. It can also be baked for a crispy texture.*

1 small red cabbage, outer leaves removed, thinly sliced

Juice of 1 lime

2 tablespoons sesame oil

2 tablespoons soy sauce

1 teaspoon garlic powder

1 ripe yet firm mango, thinly sliced

4 okra, trimmed and sliced across

Salt

Black pepper

1. Bring a large pot of water to a boil. Fill a bowl with ice water. Blanch the cabbage in the pot for about 1 minute, then transfer it immediately to the bowl of ice water to stop further cooking. Drain the cabbage on paper or kitchen towels. Transfer the cabbage to a large bowl.

2. Mix the lime juice, oil, soy sauce, and garlic powder in a small bowl. Add salt and pepper to taste.

3. Add the mango and okra to the cabbage, then add the dressing and toss to combine.

# FRESH
# PINEAPPLE SALAD

SERVES 4

**PREP TIME:** 10 minutes ✦ **REST TIME:** 1 hour

*What is more refreshing than pineapple? I was inspired by East African salads like Kachumbari
(East-African Tomato and Onion Salad, page 56) to make this salad both sweet and savory.*

½ medium pineapple, cut into
½-inch (1 cm) cubes

1 cucumber, diced

1 avocado, diced and sprinkled
with lemon juice to prevent
browning

1 red bell pepper, diced

1 red onion, diced

1 green chile pepper (such as
jalapeño), diced

½ cup (25 g) chopped cilantro
leaves

½ cup (25 g) chopped mint
leaves

**DRESSING**

¼ cup (60 ml) olive oil

2 tablespoons agave nectar

2 tablespoons fresh lime juice

1 teaspoon paprika

Salt

Black pepper

1. To make the dressing, mix the oil, agave nectar, lime juice,
   paprika, salt, and pepper in a small bowl. Whisk energetically
   for 1 minute.

2. Place the pineapple, cucumber, avocado, bell pepper, onion,
   and chile pepper in a large bowl. Add the dressing, cilantro,
   and mint. Season with salt and pepper to taste, then toss to
   combine.

3. Place in the refrigerator for 1 hour before serving.

# ROASTED CAULIFLOWER WITH PEANUT-GINGER SAUCE

SERVES 4

**PREP TIME:** 10 minutes ✦ **COOK TIME:** 45 minutes

*This recipe combines the flavors of North Africa (Morocco in particular) and sub-Saharan West Africa. It was inspired by my exchanges with Senegalese immigrants I met in Marrakech, who live their lives balancing between these two cultures.*

¼ cup (60 ml) olive oil

1 teaspoon ground cumin

1 teaspoon garlic powder

1 teaspoon smoked paprika

1 cauliflower, broken into florets

Salt

Black pepper

**PEANUT-GINGER SAUCE**

¼ cup (60g) creamy peanut butter

2 tablespoons coconut aminos or soy sauce

Juice of 1 lime

1 tablespoon maple syrup or sugar

1 teaspoon minced garlic

1 teaspoon minced ginger

Chili paste, to taste

1. Preheat the oven to 400°F (200°C).

2. Whisk together the oil, cumin, garlic powder, and paprika in a large bowl. Add the cauliflower florets and stir to coat. Sprinkle with salt and pepper.

3. Transfer to a baking sheet and roast for about 45 minutes, until tender and golden brown. If the cauliflower browns too quickly, cover with foil.

4. While the cauliflower roasts, prepare the sauce. Mix together the peanut butter, 3 tablespoons water, coconut aminos, lime juice, maple syrup, garlic, ginger, and chili paste in a small bowl.

5. Remove the cauliflower from the oven. Serve warm with the peanut-ginger sauce on the side.

# CAULIFLOWER TABBOULEH WITH PISTACHIO AND LEMON CONFIT

SERVES 4

**PREP TIME:** 20 minutes

*Here's another recipe that mixes African and Eastern flavors. Lebanese tabbouleh is typically made with lots of fresh parsley, but I wanted to incorporate cauliflower here, because it's a truly impressive vegetable. This tabbouleh can be made in seconds. It's fresh, lightly acidic, and crispy, and it can be served as a main dish or a side to grilled veggies.*

3 tablespoons olive oil

1 teaspoon coconut sugar

1 teaspoon garlic powder

Juice of 1 lemon, minced

1 white onion, diced

1 cauliflower

2 tomatoes, diced

1 cucumber, diced

1 preserved lemon

1 bunch mint, chopped

1 bunch flat-leaf parsley, chopped

½ cup (60 g) pistachios, lightly crushed

Salt

Black pepper

1. Mix the oil, sugar, garlic powder, lemon juice, and a pinch of salt together in a medium bowl. Add the onion and stir to combine.

2. Grate the cauliflower into a large bowl, stopping when you reach the stem.

3. Add the tomatoes, cucumber, preserved lemon, mint, parsley, and pistachios, then drizzle with the dressing. Season with salt and pepper and toss to combine.

# CASSAVA TABBOULEH WITH RADISHES AND HERBS

SERVES 4

**PREP TIME:** 20 minutes  ✦  **COOK TIME:** 2 hours, 15 minutes

*For generations, a large Lebanese population has made Côte d'Ivoire their home. Ivorians are very fond of dishes that come from the country of cedar trees. This tabbouleh, a combination of two iconic dishes— tabbouleh from Lebanon and attiéké from Côte d'Ivoire—is my way of paying homage to the cross-cultural sharing that makes Côte d'Ivoire so rich.*

1 small ball (14 ounces/400 g) prepared attiéké (cassava couscous)

1 bunch radishes, thinly sliced

1 bunch scallions, thinly sliced

1 bunch mint, chopped

1 bunch parsley, chopped

Juice of 1 lemon

2 tablespoons sesame oil

1 teaspoon garlic powder

Salt

Black pepper

1. Steam the attiéké for 15 minutes in a steamer or heat in a microwave for 1 to 2 minutes to reheat it. Place in a large bowl.

2. Add the radishes, scallions, mint, and parsley.

3. To make the dressing, mix the lemon juice, oil, garlic powder, salt, and pepper in a small bowl. Pour over the tabbouleh and toss to combine.

4. Serve immediately so the attiéké doesn't get soggy.

# VEGETABLE PASTELS

MAKES 8 TO 10 PASTELS

**PREP TIME:** 30 minutes  ✦  **COOK TIME:** 30 minutes

*In Côte d'Ivoire, pastels mean celebration! These little veggie pastels are my sister Monique's specialty, and she always serves them on holidays. I've always admired her skill and loved to watch her shape them by hand one by one.*

1 tablespoon olive oil, plus more for brushing

1 yellow onion, diced

1 red bell pepper, diced

1 small eggplant, diced

1 carrot, diced

1 tablespoon tomato paste

Salt

Black pepper

1 teaspoon coconut sugar

1 teaspoon garlic powder

1 teaspoon paprika

1 teaspoon dried thyme

2 parsley sprigs, chopped

1 sheet puff pastry dough

1. Heat the oil in a large skillet over medium heat. Add the onion and sauté until translucent, about 5 minutes. Reduce the heat to low, then add the pepper, eggplant, and carrot and sauté until softened, about 5 minutes, stirring occasionally.

2. Stir in the tomato paste and season with salt and pepper. Add 1 tablespoon of water and cook, stirring occasionally, until the vegetables have softened, about 15 minutes. Add the sugar, garlic powder, paprika, thyme, and parsley. Cook until all the water has evaporated, 3 to 5 minutes.

3. Preheat the oven to 400°F (200°C). Line a baking sheet with parchment paper.

4. Unroll the puff pastry and cut out circles about 4 inches (10 cm) in diameter, using a small bowl for a guide. Place about 1 tablespoon of the vegetable filling on half of each circle. Fold the other half over the filling and seal with a fork. Place on the baking sheet. Repeat with the remaining pastry dough and filling, then drizzle with oil.

5. Bake for about 25 minutes, flipping halfway through the cooking time, until golden brown.

# CREAMY CORN SOUP WITH PEANUTS

SERVES 4

**PREP TIME:** 10 minutes ✦ **COOK TIME:** 35 minutes

*This comforting soup is inspired by the many soups and stews eaten throughout Africa. Serve it with mashed foods like fufu or flatbreads like Injera (Ethiopian Flatbread; page 42) or Chapati (East African Flatbread; page 38).*

1 tablespoon olive oil

1 onion, chopped

1 garlic clove, minced

One 15-ounce (425 g) can corn, drained and rinsed

1 yellow bell pepper, diced

1 cup (240 ml) coconut milk

1 vegetable stock cube, crumbled

½ cup (75 g) roasted peanuts, crushed

Black pepper

1. Heat the oil in a heavy-bottomed saucepan over low heat. Sauté the onion and garlic until the onion is translucent, about 8 minutes. Add the corn and bell pepper and sauté until softened, 5 minutes. Add 2 cups (480 ml) water, the coconut milk, and the stock cube. Season with pepper, stir, cover, and simmer until thickened, 20 minutes.

2. Remove from the heat, let cool, then blend with a blender or immersion blender until smooth.

3. Before serving, sprinkle with the peanuts.

# CREAMY ROASTED TOMATO AND PEPPER SOUP

SERVES 6

**PREP TIME:** 20 minutes ✦ **COOK TIME:** 1 hour, 10 minutes

*I love creamy soups, especially tomato soup, because it reminds me of the spicy, comforting soups my mother would cook after the holidays. This soup can also be eaten cold in the summer, like gazpacho. It's so refreshing!*

2¼ pounds (1 kg) tomatoes, chopped

1 small sweet pepper, chopped

1 red bell pepper, chopped

2 red onions, chopped

2 carrots, chopped

3 garlic cloves, chopped

¼ cup (60 ml) olive oil, plus more for drizzling

1 tablespoon powdered sugar

4 cups (960 ml) vegetable stock

½ cup (100 g) tomato paste

Salt

Black pepper

1 teaspoon balsamic vinegar

1. Preheat the oven to 350°F (180°C). Line a baking sheet with parchment paper.

2. Place the tomatoes, peppers, onions, carrots, and garlic on the baking sheet. Drizzle with the oil, season with salt, and sprinkle with sugar.

3. Roast in the oven for about 50 minutes, until softened and browned in spots.

4. Transfer the vegetables to a large pot, add the vegetable stock and tomato paste, and simmer over low heat for 5 minutes. Let cool, then blend with a blender or immersion blender until smooth.

5. Add salt and pepper to taste, then add the balsamic vinegar and simmer for 5 minutes over low heat. Drizzle with oil before serving.

# CREAMY CARROT-GINGER SOUP

SERVES 4

**PREP TIME:** 15 minutes ✦ **COOK TIME:** 40 minutes

*There's nothing better than a warm bowl of soup in the winter. To keep nthese flavors from quickly get overused, my tip is to spice up your everyday dishes with African spices. Cacao, soumbala, chile powders . . . explore the possibilities and don't be afraid to innovate. In this soup, I use the subtle heat of ginger and the smoky flavor of cumin. Just before serving, add a few sprigs of parsley or cilantro or a few roasted cashews. It's a real treat!*

1 tablespoon coconut oil

1 red onion, chopped

1 garlic clove, chopped

1 teaspoon minced ginger

5 carrots, peeled and sliced

Salt

Black pepper

1 teaspoon ground cumin

2 cups (480 ml) vegetable stock

1 cup (240 ml) coconut milk

4 parsley or cilantro sprigs (optional)

Roasted cashews (optional)

1. Heat the oil in a heavy-bottomed pan over medium heat. Sauté the onion, garlic, and ginger until the onion is translucent, about 5 minutes. Add the carrots and sauté until soft, 10 minutes.

2. Season with salt and pepper, then add the cumin. Pour in the vegetable stock and simmer over low heat until reduced by one third, 20 minutes.

3. Blend with a blender or immersion blender, then stir in the coconut milk until creamy. Top with parsley or cashews, if desired.

# CREAMY WHITE BEAN SOUP WITH CRISPY COCONUT BACON

SERVES 4

**PREP TIME:** 15 minutes  ✦  **COOK TIME:** 30 minutes

*I ate a lot of white beans growing up, but certainly never in soup. They're more often cooked with tomato sauce for a quick meal my mother often made us. Beans cooked in sauces are a common street food in numerous East and Central African countries. They're also eaten with bread, or with beignets (see Plantain Beignets, page 28), like in Cameroon. This white bean soup is topped with crispy coconut "bacon" strips to add a little texture and a subtle smoky flavor.*

## SOUP

1 vegetable stock cube

1 tablespoon olive oil

1 yellow onion, minced

1 celery stalk, minced

2 garlic cloves, minced

1 teaspoon dried thyme

One 15.5-ounce (439 g) can white beans, drained and rinsed

Salt

Black pepper

## COCONUT BACON

2 tablespoons liquid smoke

1 tablespoon maple syrup

2 teaspoons soy sauce

½ teaspoon paprika

4 cups (500 g) dried coconut flakes

1. To make the soup, dissolve the stock cube in 4 cups (960 ml) of water in a saucepan.

2. Heat the oil in a large pot over medium heat. Add the onion, celery, and garlic and cook until softened, 10 minutes.

3. Stir in the thyme, then add 1 cup (240 ml) of the vegetable stock to the pot. Cover and simmer for 5 minutes. Add another 1 cup (240 ml) of vegetable stock, cover, and simmer for 5 minutes.

4. Add the beans and the remaining 2 cups of vegetable stock to the pot, season with salt and pepper to taste, and stir. Blend with a blender or immersion blender until creamy.

5. To make the coconut bacon, preheat the oven to 350°F (180°C). Line a baking sheet with parchment paper.

6. Mix the liquid smoke, maple syrup, soy sauce, and paprika in a large bowl. Add the coconut flakes and toss to coat.

7. Spread the coconut flakes on the baking sheet in an even layer. Bake for about 10 minutes, until browned and crunchy, like bacon. Keep an eye on them to make sure they don't burn! Let cool, then sprinkle over the soup before serving.

---

TIP: *The coconut bacon will keep in an airtight container in the fridge for 1 week. You can add them to salads or simply enjoy them as a snack.*

---

# CHILLED WATERMELON, TOMATO, AND MANGO SOUP

SERVES 4

**PREP TIME:** 10 minutes ✦ **REST TIME:** 1 hour

*Watermelon is my favorite fruit. It reminds me of weekend trips to the seaside city of Bassam, in Côte d'Ivoire. We often stopped at the markets to buy fruits and vegetables on the way. Even today, whenever I think of Côte d'Ivoire, these images of impromptu market trips, crowded stalls, and bright, fresh produce are my most vivid memories of home.*

1 small watermelon (about 1¾ pounds/800 g), seeds removed, chopped

4 tomatoes, peeled, seeds removed, chopped

1 mango, peeled and cubed

6 mint leaves

2 tablespoons olive oil

Juice of ½ lemon

1 teaspoon raspberry or white wine vinegar

Pinch of paprika

Salt

Black pepper

1. Place the watermelon, tomatoes, mango, and mint in a blender.

2. Add the oil, lemon juice, vinegar, paprika, salt, and pepper. Blend until smooth.

3. Refrigerate for at least 1 hour before serving.

# SOPA DE AMENDOIM
## Angolan Peanut Soup

SERVES 4

**PREP TIME:** 10 minutes ✦ **COOK TIME:** 15 minutes

*This tasty soup is an Angolan classic. In fact, sopa de amendoim means "peanut soup" in Portuguese, the official language of this large African country. It's fantastic as is, but you can also add cut vegetables like carrots, celery, or turnips.*

1 vegetable stock cube

1 yellow onion, chopped

1 small green bell pepper, minced

1 green chile pepper (such as jalapeño), minced

½ cup (120 g) peanut butter

Salt

Black pepper

1. Bring 4 cups (960 ml) water to a boil in a large pot. Add the stock cube and stir to dissolve, then add the onion and peppers. Cook until softened, about 10 minutes.

2. Stir in the peanut butter, then season with salt and pepper to taste.

3. Serve immediately.

# RWANDAN
# VEGETABLE SOUP

SERVES 4

**PREP TIME:** 15 minutes ✦ **COOK TIME:** 50 minutes

*Here's a naturally vegan soup from Rwanda. It's simple to make, rich in nutrients from the vegetables and rich in protein from the lentils. It's perfect for cold winter nights.*

1 tablespoon olive oil

1 onion, chopped

2 garlic cloves, chopped

2 small sweet potatoes, peeled and diced

1 carrot, diced

1 celery stalk, diced

Half a 28-ounce (794 g) can crushed tomatoes

¾ cup (140 g) green lentils, rinsed

2 vegetable stock cubes, crumbled

1 bay leaf

Pinch of dried rosemary

Pinch of dried thyme

7 ounces (200 g) spinach, chopped

Black pepper

1. Heat the oil in a large pot over medium heat, add the onions and garlic, and sauté until the onions are tender and lightly browned, about 5 minutes.

2. Add the potatoes, carrot, and celery. Stir, reduce the heat to low, and simmer for 10 minutes. Add the tomatoes, lentils, stock cubes, bay leaf, thyme, and rosemary. Stir in the spinach, season with pepper, cover with water, and mix well.

3. Simmer until the lentils are cooked through, about 40 minutes. Remove the bay leaf and enjoy while hot!

# MAIN
# DISHES

———

# PLANTAIN AND EGGPLANT STEW

### SERVES 4

**PREP TIME:** 10 minutes ✦ **COOK TIME:** 1 hour

*There's no shortage of stew recipes from one end of Africa to the other. I particularly love these all-in-one dishes because they're rich, comforting, and simple to make. You can make this stew your own by adding any vegetable you like or replacing the plantains with root vegetables like sweet potatoes or yams.*

2 tablespoons olive oil

1 yellow onion, minced

1 large eggplant, diced

1 tablespoon garlic powder

Pinch of ground cumin

Pinch of paprika

One 14.5-ounce (411 g) can crushed tomatoes

1 tablespoon tomato paste

1 bay leaf

1 teaspoon sugar

Salt

Black pepper

2 ripe, firm plantains, peeled and sliced 1½ inches (4 cm) thick

1. Heat the oil in a heavy-bottomed pot over medium heat. Add the onion and sauté until softened, about 8 minutes.

2. Add the eggplant, garlic powder, cumin, and paprika. Cook, stirring occasionally, until the eggplant is golden brown, about 10 minutes.

3. Add the tomatoes, tomato paste, bay leaf, and sugar. Season with salt and pepper, then let simmer until thickened, 30 minutes.

4. Bring a pot of salted water to a boil. Add the plantain slices and cook until tender, about 10 minutes.

5. Add the plantains to the stew and stir gently. Reduce the heat to low and cook for 5 minutes. Enjoy while hot.

# CAULIFLOWER YASSA WITH OLIVES

SERVES 4

**PREP TIME:** 15 minutes ✦ **RESTING TIME:** 1 hour ✦ **COOK TIME:** 35 minutes

*You may have already heard of yassa, the traditional Senegalese dish made with chicken or fish. Yassa is a staple of West African cuisines. This is my vegan version of it using cauliflower. Its dense texture makes it a lovely substitute for chicken. Serve this dish with white rice or Atassi (Beninese Rice and Beans, page 132).*

Juice of 1 lemon

2 tablespoons mustard

2 garlic cloves, minced

1 teaspoon freshly grated ginger

Salt

Black pepper

1 large cauliflower, chopped

6 medium onions, thinly sliced

½ cup (65 g) green olives, pitted

3 tablespoons olive oil

1 bunch parsley, chopped

1 tablespoon coconut sugar

2 bay leaves

1. Mix the lemon juice, mustard, garlic, ginger, salt, and pepper in a large bowl. Add the cauliflower, onions, and olives, and toss to coat. Let marinate for at least one hour (or overnight in the refrigerator if you prefer).

2. Remove the cauliflower from the bowl and set aside.

3. Heat 2 tablespoons of the oil in a nonstick skillet over medium heat. Add the onions and marinade mixture and cook until translucent, about 5 minutes. Add the parsley, sugar, and bay leaves, and mix well. Add 3 tablespoons water, cover, and let simmer until the onions have softened, 10 to 15 minutes.

4. Heat the remaining 1 tablespoon of oil in a frying pan over medium-high heat. Add the cauliflower and cook until tender and golden brown, 15 minutes.

5. Stir the cauliflower into the onion mixture. Adjust the salt and pepper to taste and eat while hot.

# GRILLED SQUASH
# WITH HARISSA

SERVES 4

**PREP TIME:** 15 minutes ✦ **COOK TIME:** 20 minutes

*Tiep, a classic Senegalese dish made with fish, rice, tomatoes, and onions, is often served with boiled or roasted vegetables. That's precisely what inspired this recipe. It can be served on its own or with white rice or semolina with dried fruits (such as apricots, dates, or raisins) and chopped almonds.*
*For softer raisins, soak them in tea or water for a few minutes, then pat dry.*

1 small butternut squash, halved lengthwise and sliced lengthwise

2 red onions, sliced

2 tablespoons harissa

2 tablespoons olive oil

½ bunch cilantro, chopped

1. Preheat the oven to 350°F (180°C). Line a baking sheet with parchment paper.

2. Place the squash and onions in a large bowl, add the harissa and oil, and stir to coat.

3. Transfer the slices to the baking sheet and arrange in a single layer.

4. Bake for about 20 minutes, until tender and golden brown.

5. Sprinkle with cilantro before serving.

# SAUTÉED SPINACH AND MUSHROOMS WITH PLANTAINS

SERVES 4

**PREP TIME:** 15 minutes  ✦  **COOK TIME:** 35 minutes

*Dishes made with leafy greens are very popular in sub-Saharan Africa, particularly in South and Central Africa. Any leafy green will do—such as taro, cassava, sorrel, or sweet potato leaves—but here I opted for spinach leaves, since they're easy to find in most parts of the world.*

2 tablespoons vegetable oil

1 onion, chopped

4 tomatoes, diced

8 ounces (225 g) button mushrooms, chopped

3⅓ pounds (1.5 kg) spinach

4 ripe, firm plantains, peeled and cut into large chunks

1 vegetable stock cube, crumbled

2 teaspoons garlic powder

Salt

Black pepper

1. Heat the oil in a large frying pan over medium heat. Add the onion and cook until translucent and lightly browned, about 5 minutes. Stir in the tomatoes and cook, stirring regularly, for about 5 minutes.

2. Add the mushrooms and stir to combine. Add the spinach gradually, stirring to wilt, then stir in the stock cube, garlic powder, salt, and pepper. Bring to a simmer, cover, and cook, stirring occasionally, until thickened, for about 10 minutes. If the mixture sticks to the pan, stir in a splash of water.

3. Meanwhile, place the plantains in a large pot, cover with salted water, and bring to a boil. Cook until easily pierced with a fork, about 15 minutes.

4. Serve the spinach and mushrooms along with the plantains.

TIP: *To steam the plantains, make a small cut halfway through each piece. Place in a steamer and steam until easily pierced with a fork, about 10 minutes.*

# GRILLED VEGETABLE WRAPS

SERVES 4

**PREP TIME:** 20 minutes ✦ **COOK TIME:** 35 minutes

*This vegetable wrap is perfect for repurposing leftovers. Don't be afraid to make them with whatever you have on hand. This is another tribute to Ivorian street food where shawarma and pain-chien (an Ivorian beef sandwich on crusty bread) are king.*

1 medium sweet potato, chopped

1 red bell pepper, chopped

1 yellow bell pepper, chopped

10 cherry tomatoes, halved

Coconut oil

1 teaspoon ground allspice

1 teaspoon garlic powder

1 teaspoon smoked paprika

4 whole wheat wraps

Handful of mesclun greens

1 avocado, sliced

2 tablespoons chopped cilantro

Salt

Black pepper

1. Preheat the oven to 350°F (180°C). Line a baking sheet with parchment paper.

2. Place the sweet potato, red and yellow bell peppers, and tomatoes on the baking sheet. Drizzle with oil, and sprinkle with the allspice, garlic powder, and paprika. Season with salt and pepper to taste, then stir well to coat.

3. Roast for 35 minutes or until the vegetables are golden brown. Remove from the baking sheet and let cool completely.

4. Heat the wraps in the still-hot oven for 1 minute.

5. Add the roasted vegetables, mesclun greens, and avocado to the wraps, then top with cilantro.

TIP: *Spread some Peanut Hummus (page 22) on your wraps and add a dash of olive oil for even more flavor.*

# CREAMY AVOCADO RISOTTO

SERVES 4

**PREP TIME:** 5 minutes ✦ **COOK TIME:** 30 minutes

*Though rice is eaten throughout Africa, risotto isn't quite an authentic African recipe. I wanted to "Africanize" risotto with the addition of avocado. The result? A creamy, flavorful meal. Enrich this dish by adding roasted pistachios just before serving for texture and crunch.*

2 tablespoons olive oil

1 yellow onion, chopped

1 garlic clove, minced

1 cup (200 g) arborio rice

2½ cups (600 ml) vegetable broth

Juice of 1 lemon

1 avocado, mashed

Roasted pistachios (optional)

Salt

Black pepper

1. Heat the oil in a large pot over medium heat. Sauté the onion and garlic until the onion is translucent, about 8 minutes.

2. Add the rice and stir until translucent, 2 minutes. Add the broth, reduce the heat to low, and simmer until the liquid has been absorbed, 20 minutes. Stir regularly to prevent the rice from sticking to the bottom.

3. Add the lemon juice, avocado, and pistachios if desired. Season with salt and pepper to taste, and enjoy immediately.

# MILLET WITH ROASTED TOMATOES

SERVES 4

**PREP TIME:** 20 minutes ✦ **COOK TIME:** 40 minutes ✦ **RESTING TIME:** 10 minutes

*Millet is a very common cereal in sub-Saharan Africa, where it's prepared with sauces, as porridge, or in fritters. For a long time, I ate only sweet millet dishes; one of my favorites was a comforting millet porridge with ginger. Recently, however, I've been enjoying it with grilled or roasted vegetables for an easy, delicious, and nutritious meal. Millet is a good source of vitamins B and E, iron and zinc, silica, phosphorus, and magnesium and also an excellent source of fiber.*

4 tomatoes, quartered

1 large red onion, diced

1 garlic clove, chopped

⅓ cup (80 ml) olive oil

Salt

Black pepper

1 cup (200 g) millet, rinsed

Juice of 1 lemon

1 tablespoon chopped mint

1 tablespoon chopped parsley

1. Preheat the oven to 400°F (200°C). Line a baking dish with parchment paper.

2. Place the tomatoes, onion, and garlic in the baking dish, drizzle with a little oil, and season with salt and pepper. Roast for 30 minutes, until golden brown. Transfer to a large bowl.

3. Meanwhile, place the millet in a pot with 2 cups (480 ml) salted water. Stir, bring to a boil, reduce the heat to low, cover, and simmer until the liquid is absorbed, 10 minutes. Remove from the heat and let stand for 10 minutes.

4. Uncover the pot and fluff the millet with a fork. Add the millet to the roasted vegetables and stir.

5. Combine the lemon juice, the remaining oil, the mint, and parsley in a small bowl, then pour the mixture over the millet and vegetables. Toss to combine and serve.

# POTATO STEW
# WITH OLIVES

SERVES 4

**PREP TIME:** 15 minutes  ✦  **COOK TIME:** 1 hour

*This Moroccan-influenced stew, inspired by a family recipe, is one of my favorites. Sometimes, I also like to add sun-dried tomatoes or roasted red peppers.*

2 tablespoons olive oil

1 large onion, minced

One 14.5-ounce (411 g) can crushed tomatoes

½ cup (65 g) green olives, pitted

2 garlic cloves, minced

1 teaspoon tomato paste

1 teaspoon ground cumin

1 teaspoon smoked paprika

1 teaspoon cane sugar

1 teaspoon ground turmeric

Harissa paste, to taste

8 medium potatoes (about 3 pounds/1.3 kg), quartered

A few cilantro sprigs, chopped

Salt

Black pepper

1. Heat the oil in a large pot over medium-high heat. Add the onion and cook until lightly browned, about 8 minutes. Add the tomatoes, olives, garlic, tomato paste, cumin, paprika, sugar, turmeric, and harissa paste. Season with salt and pepper, stir, and simmer over low heat until reduced slightly, 20 minutes.

2. Add the potatoes, along with a splash of water. Cover and simmer over low heat until the potatoes are cooked through, 30 minutes. Sprinkle with cilantro before serving.

# CHAKALAKA
## South African Relish

SERVES 4

**PREP TIME:** 10 minutes ✦ **COOK TIME:** 40 minutes

*Chakalaka is a traditional South African dish. It's deliciously spiced and typically served with white rice, fish, or even meat. But no need for these last few. Chakalaka is delicious on its own, and just as good eaten cold as it is warm.*

2 tablespoons olive oil

2 yellow onions, minced

1 garlic clove, minced

2 teaspoons curry powder

1 teaspoon grated ginger

1 teaspoon paprika or ¼ teaspoon cayenne

1 teaspoon smoked paprika

1 teaspoon dried thyme

1 green bell pepper, chopped

1 red bell pepper, chopped

2 carrots, grated

3 small tomatoes, chopped

1 teaspoon tomato paste

Salt

Half a 15.5-ounce (439 g) can chickpeas, drained and rinsed

Half a 15.5-ounce (439 g) can white beans, drained and rinsed

½ bunch cilantro, chopped (optional)

Black pepper

1. Heat the oil in a large frying pan over medium heat, then add the onions and garlic. Cook until the onions are translucent, about 5 minutes.

2. Stir in the curry powder, ginger, paprika, smoked paprika, and thyme. Add the green and red bell peppers, carrots, tomatoes, and tomato paste. Season with salt, stir again, and cover the pan. Simmer to thicken over low heat, 30 minutes.

3. Uncover the pan, add the chickpeas and white beans and stir. Cover and simmer for 5 minutes.

4. Season with salt and pepper to taste, and top with cilantro just before serving.

# SWEET POTATO AND KIDNEY BEAN STEW

SERVES 4

**PREP TIME:** 20 minutes ✦ **COOK TIME:** 30 Minutes

*This stew can be eaten on its own or with rice, particularly Jollof Rice (page 130). It can also be enjoyed as leftovers, when the flavor of the spices has really developed. In some ways, that's even better! It has become one of my favorite dishes.*

1 tablespoon coconut oil

1 red onion, chopped

1 large red bell pepper, diced

4 garlic cloves, minced

2 teaspoons ground coriander

2 teaspoons ground cumin

2 teaspoons smoked paprika

1 teaspoon paprika or
¼ teaspoon cayenne

¼ teaspoon ground allspice

Salt

Black pepper

2 large sweet potatoes, peeled and cut into 1-inch (2.5 cm) cubes

Two 15-ounce (411 g) cans red kidney beans

One 28-ounce (794 g) can crushed tomatoes

1 tablespoon tomato paste

2 teaspoons coconut sugar

1 cup (240 ml) vegetable stock

½ bunch cilantro, chopped

1 scallion, chopped

1. Heat the oil in a pot over medium heat. Add the onion and cook until translucent, stirring frequently, 5 minutes.

2. Add the bell pepper, garlic, coriander, cumin, smoked paprika, paprika, and allspice. Add salt and pepper to taste, then stir and cook until the vegetables are softened, 5 minutes. If the mixture begins to stick to the bottom of the pot, add a splash of water.

3. Add the sweet potatoes. Stir well, then add the beans, tomatoes, tomato paste, and sugar. Add the vegetable stock and stir well to combine. Reduce the heat to low, cover, and simmer until the potatoes are soft and the vegetable stock is reduced, 20 minutes. Top with cilantro and scallion before serving.

# EGUSI STEW
## African Pistachio Stew

SERVES 4

**PREP TIME:** 15 minutes ✦ **COOK TIME:** 45 minutes

*Egusi Stew is a Nigerian dish traditionally served with "swallows," a starchy paste made of pounded yam, cassava, plantain, fufu, or other foods. Egusi is eaten with your hands, using a swallow to scoop up the stew. You can replace the swallow with rice, yam, or plantains.*

3 tomatoes, chopped

1 bell pepper, chopped

⅓ Scotch bonnet pepper or small sweet pepper, seeds removed

3 garlic cloves, chopped

2 tablespoons red palm oil

1 large yellow onion, chopped

4 ounces (100 g) egusi (African pistachios), ground

1 cup (240 ml) vegetable stock

1 tablespoon paprika

1 teaspoon curry powder

1 teaspoon tomato paste

1 teaspoon dried thyme

18 ounces (510 g) fresh spinach

4 ounces (113 g) oyster mushrooms

Salt

Black pepper

1. Place the tomatoes, bell pepper, Scotch bonnet pepper, and garlic in a food processor and process to form a smooth paste. If necessary, add a splash of water.

2. Heat the oil in a large pot over medium heat. Add half of the chopped onion and cook until translucent, 5 minutes. Add the tomato mixture, paprika, curry powder, tomato paste, and thyme. Stir, cover, and cook until thickened, 15 minutes.

3. Meanwhile, mix the egusi, the remaining chopped onion, and ½ cup of the vegetable stock together in a medium bowl.

4. Add the egusi mixture to the pot and cook until thickened, 10 minutes. Add the spinach, mushrooms, and remaining ½ cup of vegetable stock. Add salt and pepper to taste, reduce the heat to low, cover the pot, and simmer until creamy, 10 minutes. Enjoy hot.

# YAM AKPESSI
## Ivorian Eggplant and Yam

SERVES 4

**PREP TIME:** 30 minutes ✦ **COOK TIME:** 1 hour

*Akpessi is an Ivorian eggplant-based dish traditionally made with smoked fish. Here is my delicious vegan version. You can eat it with plantains, yam, or cassava.*

12 African or 2 Italian eggplants, peeled and chopped (see Note)

2 tomatoes

1 small sweet red pepper or habanero chile pepper

2 yellow onions

2 garlic cloves

2 tablespoons vegetable oil

1 teaspoon grated ginger

2 tablespoons tomato paste

1 vegetable stock cube, crumbled

1 yam, peeled and chopped

Salt

Black pepper

1. Bring a large pot of water to a boil. Add the eggplants and cook them until tender, 15 minutes.

2. Slice a shallow "X" into the bottom of each tomato. When the eggplants have been cooking for 5 minutes, add the tomatoes and cook them for the remaining 10 minutes. Strain the eggplants and tomatoes and let cool.

3. Peel and chop the tomatoes, then place the tomatoes, eggplants, and red pepper in a food processor and purée until smooth. Transfer to a bowl.

4. Cut the first onion in chunks. Place it and the garlic in the food processor and purée until smooth. Chop the second onion.

5. Heat the oil in a large pot over medium heat and add the minced onion. Cook until softened, about 5 minutes. Add the eggplant purée, onion purée, ginger, tomato paste, stock cube, and ½ cup (120 ml) water. Stir, reduce the heat to low, and simmer, stirring occasionally, until thickened, 20 minutes.

6. Meanwhile, place the yam in a large pot and cover with water. Season with salt, bring to a boil, and cook until easily pierced with a fork, 20 minutes.

7. Season the stew with salt and pepper to taste. Serve with the boiled yam on the side.

TIP: *African eggplants are small, round, and white. Italian eggplants are large, long, and purple.*

# ATAKILT WAT
## Ethiopian Cabbage, Potatoes, and Carrots

SERVES 4

**PREP TIME:** 20 minutes ✦ **COOK TIME:** 25 minutes

*The most popular dish in Ethiopia is wat (ወጥ), a stew made with vegetables, pulses, or some kind of meat. Atakilt Wat is a simple variation that's both delicious and traditionally vegan. And like most Ethiopian stews, serve it with Injera (Ethiopian Flatbread, page 42).*

2 tablespoons olive oil

1 yellow onion, minced

2 garlic cloves, minced

1 teaspoon grated ginger

½ teaspoon ground cardamom

½ teaspoon ground cinnamon

½ teaspoon ground cumin

½ teaspoon ground turmeric

4 potatoes, peeled and chopped

4 carrots, peeled and chopped

½ green cabbage, chopped

Salt

Black pepper

1. Heat the oil in a frying pan over medium heat, add the onion, garlic, and grated ginger, and cook until the onion is softened, 3 minutes.

2. Add the cardamom, cinnamon, cumin, and turmeric, and stir for 1 to 2 minutes. Add ⅔ cup (160 ml) water, stir to loosen the onions, and add the potatoes, carrots, and cabbage, and season with salt and pepper.

3. Cover the pot and cook, stirring occasionally, until the potatoes are cooked through, 20 minutes. Enjoy while hot.

# RED RED
## Ghanian Red Stew

SERVES 4

**PREP TIME:** 10 minutes ✦ **COOK TIME:** 1 hour, 30 minutes

*The aptly named "Red Red," eaten at all hours of the day, is iconic Ghanaian street food. It takes its name from the red palm oil used in it, but also from the fried plantains which often accompany it. Here, I've replaced the fried plantains with avocado slices.*

7 ounces (200 g) black-eyed peas

¼ cup (60 ml) red palm oil (or argan oil)

1 large red onion, minced

2 garlic cloves, minced

One 1.5-inch (4 cm) piece of ginger, minced

1 tablespoon tomato paste

4 ripe tomatoes, chopped

2 habanero chile peppers or small sweet peppers

2 cups (480 ml) vegetable stock

Sliced avocado

Flat-leaf parsley sprigs, chopped

Salt

Black pepper

1. Soak the black-eyed peas in hot water for 30 minutes. Place the beans in a large pot and cover with water. Bring to a boil, reduce to a simmer, and cook until tender, 30 to 40 minutes.

2. Heat the oil in a frying pan over medium-high heat. Add the onion, garlic, and ginger and cook until tender and lightly caramelized, 3 to 4 minutes. Stir in the tomato paste, add the tomatoes and habaneros, stir for 1 minute, and cook for 10 minutes.

3. Add the black-eyed peas and vegetable stock to the pan, reduce the heat to low, and simmer until creamy, 30 minutes.

4. Season with salt and pepper to taste, then top with avocado and parsley and serve.

TIP: *To make the black-eyed peas softer and easier to digest, soak them in cold water overnight.*

# BOBOTIE
## South African Casserole

SERVES 4

**PREP TIME:** 45 minutes ◆ **COOK TIME:** 1 hour, 15 minutes

*Bobotie, a well-known South African dish similar to the French Hachis Parmentier, is traditionally made with meat. It's a very comforting dish, both sweet and salty from the presence of dried fruits. It's typically served with Geelrys (South African Yellow Rice with Raisins, page 128) and vegetables. Bobotie was brought to Africa in the seventeenth century from Indonesia and adapted by the Cape Malays, descendants of slaves and political deportees from Indonesia and Malaysia.*

Vegetable oil

1½ cups (300 g) green lentils

2 onions, minced

3 carrots, chopped

1 cup (115 g) walnuts, chopped

2 apples, grated

1 cup (150 g) raisins

3 tablespoons apricot jam

2 garlic cloves, minced

1 tablespoon soy sauce

2 teaspoons ground cinnamon

2 teaspoons ground cumin

1½ teaspoons black pepper

½ teaspoon ground cloves

½ teaspoon paprika

½ teaspoon ground turmeric

Juice of 1 lemon

Zest of 1 lemon

2 slices whole wheat bread

¾ cup (180 ml) plant milk (like almond or soy)

Salt

### SAUCE

¾ cup (90 g) chickpea flour

1 teaspoon baking powder

½ teaspoon ground turmeric

¼ teaspoon salt

1 cup (240 ml) plant milk

2 bay leaves

1. Preheat the oven to 350°F (180°C). Grease a baking dish with oil.

2. Place the lentils in a medium pot and with 4 cups (960 ml) water. Bring to a boil, reduce the heat to a very low simmer, and cook the lentils until tender but not mushy, 18 to 20 minutes. Drain and set aside to cool. When cooled, mash them and stir with a fork to form a slightly rough texture.

3. Heat a thin layer of oil in a frying pan over medium heat. Add the onions and cook until translucent, 5 minutes. Mix the carrots and walnuts together in a medium bowl, then add them to the pan, along with the lentils. Stir to combine and cook the mixture until softened, 5 minutes.

4. Add the apples, raisins, jam, garlic, soy sauce, cinnamon, cumin, black pepper, cloves, paprika, and turmeric. Add the lemon juice, lemon zest, and salt to taste. Reduce the heat to low and cook the lentil mixture until the liquid has evaporated, 5 minutes.

5. Soak the bread slices in the milk. When the slices are soft, use a fork to transfer them to the pan. Stir gently to incorporate them into the lentil mixture. Transfer the mixture to the baking dish, then pack and smooth the surface.

6. To make the sauce, mix together the flour, baking powder, turmeric, and salt in a small bowl, then slowly stir in the milk. Pour it over the lentil mixture, add the bay leaves, and bake in the oven for 20 to 30 minutes, until golden brown.

---

TIP: *Sprinkle the top of the Bobotie with bread crumbs before baking, for a nice crunchy texture.*

# GARI FOTO
## Togan Cassava with Tomato

**PREP TIME:** 15 minutes ◆ **COOK TIME:** 25 minutes

*Gari is a fermented, coarse flour made from cassava, the root vegetable, and is used as a base ingredient in several West and Central African countries. It can be made sweet or savory. This version is a savory gari, flavored with tomato. It is sometimes eaten for breakfast, as a snack, or as a side dish.*

2 tablespoons canola oil

1 yellow onion, chopped

2 fresh tomatoes, diced

1 carrot, peeled and diced

1 green bell pepper, diced

1 teaspoon paprika

1¼ cup (300 ml) vegetable stock

¾ cup (105 g) gari (cassava flour)

1. Heat the oil in a medium pot over medium heat, then add the onion and tomatoes. Cook until softened, 5 minutes

2. Add the carrot and cook until softened, stirring constantly, for 5 minutes. Add the bell pepper, paprika, and vegetable stock. Reduce the heat to low, cover, and simmer until the vegetables are softened, 10 minutes.

3. Add the cassava flour little by little, stirring constantly, until all the liquid is absorbed, about 5 minutes. Serve hot.

# YASSA BURGER

SERVES 4

**PREP TIME:** 15 minutes  ✦  **COOK TIME:** 15 minutes

*This burger is the ultimate comfort food. It combines the pleasure of eating with your hands, with the joy that comes from tasting all these delicious African flavors. Eating with your hands is a part of my ancestral heritage. I like to do it because it's a very natural, noble way to eat. For some dishes, like attiéké (cassava couscous; see page 64), this takes a certain mastery that only comes from practice. So, let's get to it!*

1 tablespoon olive oil

1 red onion, minced

Juice of ½ lemon

1 teaspoon coconut sugar

½ teaspoon dried thyme

Salt

Black pepper

2 tablespoons coconut oil

1 ripe plantain, thinly sliced

½ teaspoon paprika

8 thick slices Sweet Bread
  (page 41), toasted

4 Red Bean Cakes (page 25)

1 red bell pepper, thinly sliced

1 avocado, peeled and sliced

Handful of spinach sprouts

1. Heat the olive oil in a large pot over low heat. Add the onion and cook until beginning to soften, 3 minutes. Add the lemon juice, sugar, thyme, salt, and pepper, increase the heat to medium, then cover and simmer until the onion has softened completely, 5 minutes. If the onion still isn't soft, add a splash of water and cook for a few more minutes. Stir frequently until the water evaporates.

2. Heat the coconut oil in a frying pan, Season the plantain slices with salt and paprika, and cook them until lightly caramelized, 2 to 3 minutes per side.

3. To assemble the burger, place a slice of toast on a plate, then top with onions, a red bean cake, plantains, red bell pepper, avocado, and spinach shoots. Finish with a slice of toast on top. Repeat to make four burgers, and serve hot.

# GITHERI
## Kenyan Corn and Bean Stew

SERVES 4

**PREP TIME:** 10 minutes ✦ **COOK TIME:** 30 minutes

*Githeri, also called muthere or mutheri, is a traditional Kenyan dish. It can be eaten on its own or with boiled potatoes or ugali, a popular corn or millet porridge found (under different names) in several East African countries.*

2 tablespoons canola oil

1 onion, minced

1 garlic clove, minced

One and a half 15.5-ounce (439 g) cans red beans, drained and rinsed

1 large tomato, chopped

1 cup (170 g) canned corn, drained and rinsed

2 teaspoons paprika

½ teaspoon curry powder

½ teaspoon white pepper

Salt

2 scallions, minced

1½ cups (360 ml) water

2 tablespoons chopped cilantro leaves

1. Heat the oil in a frying pan over medium heat. Add the onions and garlic and cook until beginning to soften, 3 minutes.

2. Add the beans, tomato, corn, paprika, curry powder, and pepper. Season with salt and stir to combine the mixture. Add 1½ cups (360 ml) water and bring to a boil. Lower the heat and simmer for 20 minutes, stirring occasionally.

3. Add the cilantro leaves just before serving.

# VEGETABLE MAFE
## Malian Peanut Stew

**PREP TIME:** 30 minutes ◆ **COOK TIME:** 1 hour, 45 minutes

*Mafe, or tiga dégué, is one of the most well-known West African dishes. I find it addictive, and if you've already eaten it, I'm sure you know what I mean. Like all traditional African dishes, there are many different recipes. Don't hesitate to make it in large batches. It's even better reheated the next day. It can also be eaten with white rice.*

2 tablespoons argan oil (or other vegetable oil)

2 onions, minced

4 garlic cloves, minced

1 teaspoon grated ginger

1 cup (260 g) canned crushed tomatoes

2 vegetable stock cubes, crumbled

¾ cup (195 g) peanut butter

3 African eggplants or 1 small Italian eggplant, peeled and chopped

1 sweet potato, peeled and chopped

½ green cabbage, chopped

3 carrots, peeled and diced

2 turnips, peeled and chopped

1 habanero chile pepper or small sweet pepper

12 okra, trimmed and chopped

Chopped peanuts (optional)

Salt

Black pepper

1. Heat the oil in a large pot over medium heat. Add the onion, garlic, and ginger, and cook until the onion is translucent, 5 minutes. Stir in the tomato paste and stock cubes, then add 6 cups (1.5 L) water and simmer over low heat for 10 minutes.

2. Add the peanut butter and stir until it is fully incorporated. Add the eggplants, sweet potato, cabbage, carrots, turnips, and habanero. Stir carefully to avoid crushing the habanero.

3. Reduce the heat to low, cover, and cook until thickened, 1 hour.

4. Add the okra, season with salt and pepper, and stir. Cook until the vegetables are soft, 30 minutes.

5. Remove the chile pepper, sprinkle with peanuts if desired, and serve.

# GRATITUDE BOWL

SERVES 2

**PREP TIME:** 25 minutes ✦ **COOK TIME:** 30 minutes

*The rule with bowls is that there are no rules. Add your favorite ingredients or whatever makes you feel good. You can sub out white rice for brown rice or another grain of your choice. For this dish, I always say that the presentation is as important as the ingredients. I often serve this dish in a calabash bowl, a container made from the hard shell of a gourd, which can also be used in spiritual practice.*

1 tablespoon olive oil

6 okra, trimmed and halved lengthwise

1 teaspoon ground cumin

Salt

Black pepper

1 ripe plantain, peeled and thinly sliced

1 teaspoon paprika

1 tablespoon coconut oil

¼ cup (50 g) white rice, drained and rinsed

1 avocado, peeled and sliced

1 beet, cooked and diced

1 small sweet pepper, seeded and chopped (optional)

½ cup (75 g) roasted peanuts

½ cup (15 g) chopped cilantro

½ cup (15 g) chopped mint

## DRESSING

Juice of 1 lime

2 tablespoons sesame oil

1 tablespoon agave nectar

1 tablespoon soy sauce

1 teaspoon minced garlic

1 teaspoon grated ginger

Salt

Black pepper

1. Heat the olive oil in a frying pan over medium heat, then add the okra, cumin, salt, and pepper. Lightly brown the okra on each side for about 5 minutes.

2. Season the plantain slices with paprika and salt. Heat the coconut oil in a frying pan and cook the plantain until caramelized, about 2 minutes on each side.

3. Place the rice in a small pot with ½ cup (120 ml) water. Bring to a boil and season with salt, then reduce the heat to low, cover, and cook until the rice is tender and the water is completely absorbed, about 10 minutes.

4. To make the dressing, mix the lime juice, sesame oil, agave, soy sauce, garlic, and ginger in a small bowl. Season with salt and pepper.

5. To assemble the bowls, place the rice in the center and arrange the okra, plantain, avocado, and beet around it.

6. Drizzle with the dressing, then top with chile pepper (if desired), peanuts, cilantro, and mint before serving.

# KEY SIR ALICIA
## Ethiopian Beet and Potato Stew

SERVES 4

**PREP TIME:** 15 minutes ✦ **COOK TIME:** 50 minutes

*Key Sir Alicia is a very simple, nutritious Ethiopian dish. It's often eaten with Injera (Ethiopian Flatbread, page 42) or on its own for a light meal.*

2 tablespoons canola oil

1 yellow onion, minced

1½ teaspoons minced garlic

1½ teaspoons grated ginger

1 teaspoon mustard seeds

½ teaspoon fenugreek seeds (optional)

2 large beets, peeled and diced

4 large potatoes, peeled and diced

1 teaspoon lemon juice

1 bunch cilantro, leaves chopped

Salt

Black pepper

1. Heat the oil in a large pot over medium heat. Add the onion and cook until translucent, 5 minutes. Add the garlic, ginger, mustard seeds, and fenugreek seeds. Stir for 1 minute.

2. Add the beets and 1 cup (240 ml) water. Season with salt and pepper, then bring to a boil. Reduce the heat to low, cover, and simmer until the beets are softened but not completely cooked, 20 to 25 minutes. Stir occasionally.

3. Rinse the diced potatoes under cold water. Add them to the pot, then cover and cook until the beets and potatoes are tender but not falling apart, 15 minutes.

4. Adjust the salt and pepper to taste, then drizzle with lemon juice and top with cilantro.

# IRIO
## Potato, Pea, and Corn Purée

SERVES 4

**PREP TIME:** 10 minutes  ✦  **COOK TIME:** 15 minutes

*Irio means "food" in the Kikuyu community in Kenya, where this simple dish is well-loved.*

5 large potatoes, peeled and cubed

Half a 15-ounce (425 g) can peas, drained and rinsed

Half a 15-ounce (425 g) can corn, drained and rinsed

Salt

Black pepper

1. Place the potatoes in a large pot, season with salt, and cover with hot water. Cook on medium heat until easily pierced with a fork, about 15 minutes. Drain, reserving 2 tablespoons of potato water.

2. Put the potatoes in a large bowl. Add the peas and mash them together, using a potato masher. Add the corn and 1 to 2 tablespoons of the reserved potato water to the potatoes and stir.

3. Season with salt and pepper, and serve hot.

# ETOR
## Ghanaian Banana Purée

SERVES 4 SERVINGS

**PREP TIME:** 30 minutes  ✦  **COOK TIME:** 15 minutes

*I've included this recipe as a tribute to my dad, who comes from Akan in Ghana. Etor (or otor) is an important cultural meal in Ghana. It has spiritual significance and is served at almost all large Ghanaian celebrations. It's often served with hard-boiled eggs and peanuts, and sometimes with pears or avocados. You can replace the ripe plantain with a green one or a yam.*

4 ripe plantains, peeled and sliced

2 tablespoons canola oil

1 yellow onion, minced

4 shallots, chopped

1 red habanero chile pepper or small sweet pepper, chopped

¼ cup (65 g) peanut butter

⅓ cup (50 g) peanuts, plus more for serving

1 avocado, peeled and sliced

1 scallion, chopped

Salt

1. Place the plantain slices in a large pot and cover them with water. Bring to a boil and let cook until soft, 10 minutes. Drain them, put them in a bowl, and mash with a potato masher or a mortar and pestle. Set aside.

2. Heat the oil in a frying pan over medium heat, then add half of the minced onion and cook until translucent, 3 minutes. Reserve.

3. Mash the rest of the minced onion, the shallots, and the habanero with a mortar and pestle or in a food processor to form a smooth paste.

4. Add the smooth vegetable paste to the plantains and mix well, then stir in the peanut butter and peanuts. Mash again, leaving some peanuts whole for texture. Add salt to taste.

5. Form the mixture into a ball. Put on a serving plate, and place the reserved sautéed onion on top.

6. Place the sliced avocado on the side and top with chopped scallion and peanuts. Enjoy!

# RICE

—

# VERMICELLI RICE WITH SPINACH AND CASHEWS

SERVES 4

**PREP TIME:** 15 minutes  ✦  **COOK TIME:** 30 minutes

*Vermicelli rice is a dish of Lebanese origin that has been integrated into West African cuisines. This recipe is based on one that I learned from my mom, but I've added spinach to make it my own.*

½ cup (65 g) cashews

¼ cup (60 ml) olive oil

3 scallions, chopped

2 garlic cloves, chopped

1¼ cup (250 g) white basmati rice, drained and rinsed

4 ounces (115 g) vermicelli

2 teaspoons curry powder

1 teaspoon grated ginger

1 teaspoon coconut sugar

1 vegetable stock cube, crumbled

14 ounces (400 g) fresh spinach

2 teaspoons chopped parsley

1. Heat a dry skillet over medium-high heat and lightly toast the cashews for about 2 minutes.

2. Heat the oil in a frying pan over medium heat, add the scallions and garlic, and cook until softened, 5 minutes. Add the rice, vermicelli, curry powder, ginger, sugar, and stock cube, and stir. Add 2½ cups (600 ml) water, and bring to a boil. Cover and let cook for 3 minutes on high heat, then reduce the heat to low and cook for 7 minutes, until the rice is tender and has absorbed the water.

3. Five minutes before the rice is ready, stir in the spinach and parsley. Add the roasted cashews just before serving.

# RICE WITH GREEN LENTILS AND ONION

SERVES 4

**PREP TIME:** 5 minutes ✦ **COOK TIME:** 25 minutes

*This simple rice and lentil dish is excellent served with vegetables, oven-roasted plantains, and sliced avocado. It's delicious!*

2 tablespoons coconut oil

1 large onion, minced

2 garlic cloves, minced

1 tablespoon ground coriander

2 teaspoons curry powder

1 teaspoon ground ginger

1 teaspoon ground nutmeg

1 teaspoon sugar

1¼ cups (250 g) cooked green lentils

1 cup (200 g) long-grain white rice

Salt

Black pepper

1. Heat the oil in a large pot over medium heat. Add the onion and cook until translucent, 5 minutes. Add the garlic, coriander, curry powder, ginger, nutmeg, and sugar. Reduce the heat to low and cook until the garlic and spices are fragrant, 2 minutes, stirring constantly. Stir in the lentils.

2. Place the rice and 2 cups (480 ml) salted water in a small pot. Bring to a boil, then reduce the heat to low. Cover the pot and cook until the rice is tender and has absorbed all the water, 15 minutes.

3. Add the rice to the onion and lentil mixture. Season with salt and pepper to taste and serve.

# GEELRYS
## South African Yellow Rice with Raisins

SERVES 4

**PREP TIME:** 5 minutes ✦ **COOK TIME:** 15 minutes

*This sweet and savory South African rice is a classic accompaniment to Bobotie*
*(South African Casserole, page 106).*

1 cup (200 g) basmati rice,
  drained and rinsed

⅔ cup (100 g) raisins

2 tablespoons vegetable oil

1 tablespoon brown sugar

1 teaspoon ground cinnamon

1 teaspoon coriander seeds

1 teaspoon garlic powder

1 teaspoon ground turmeric

1 star anise

Salt

Black pepper

1. Place the rice, raisins, oil, sugar, cinnamon, coriander, garlic powder, turmeric, and star anise in large pot. Add 2 cups (480 ml) water, season with salt and pepper, and mix well.

2. Cover the pot and bring to a boil, then lower the heat and cook until the rice is tender and has absorbed all the water, about 10 minutes.

# JOLLOF RICE

## SERVES 4

**PREP TIME:** 15 minutes  ◆  **COOK TIME:** 1 hour, 5 minutes

*For ages, Ghana and Nigeria have argued over the origins of this recipe, each claiming to make the most delicious version. In reality, it seems that the dish actually originated in Senegal!*

2 Roma tomatoes, chopped

1 red bell pepper, chopped

1 habanero chile pepper or small sweet pepper, washed and seeded

2 tablespoons olive oil

1 onion, chopped

3 garlic cloves, chopped

1 teaspoon grated ginger

1 tablespoon curry powder

1 teaspoon smoked paprika

1 teaspoon dried rosemary

1 teaspoon dried thyme

2 bay leaves

Salt

Black pepper

2 cups (400 g) brown rice

2 cups (480 ml) vegetable stock

1. Mix the tomatoes, red bell pepper, habanero, and half of the chopped onion together in a small bowl.

2. Heat the oil in a large pot over medium heat, add the other half of the chopped onion, and cook until translucent, about 3 minutes.

3. Add the garlic and ginger to the pot, then stir for about 30 seconds. Add the curry powder, paprika, rosemary, thyme, and bay leaves. Stir for 15 seconds, then stir in the tomato mixture. Season with salt and pepper, then cover and cook for 10 minutes.

4. Add the rice and vegetable stock and stir well to incorporate. Cover (see Tip), reduce the heat to low, and cook until the rice is soft and reddish-orange in color, 40 minutes.

5. Lower the heat to minimum flame and cook the rice for 10 minutes. Remove from the heat.

TIP: *To ensure evenly cooked rice, cover the pot with parchment paper before placing the lid back on in step 4.*

# PILAU RICE

SERVES 4

**PREP TIME:** 10 minutes ✦ **COOK TIME:** 30 minutes

*Pilau Rice is an East African staple, originating in India and brought to the region by migrating Indians. This version includes peppers, tomatoes, onion, and cashews, as well as a variety of fragrant spices.*

2 tablespoons canola oil

1 teaspoon ground cumin

1 teaspoon curry powder

½ teaspoon ground cardamom

½ teaspoon smoked paprika

½ teaspoon white peppercorns

1 cinnamon stick

1 star anise

1 bay leaf

1 cayenne pepper, chopped

1 onion, chopped

2 garlic cloves, chopped

1 teaspoon grated ginger

2 tomatoes, chopped

1 red bell pepper, chopped

1½ cups (300g) white basmati rice

1½ cups (360 ml) vegetable stock

1 cup (240 ml) coconut milk

Salt

Black pepper

¾ cup (100 g) cashews

1. Heat the oil in a large pot over medium heat, add the cumin, curry powder, cardamom, paprika, and peppercorns, and stir. Add the cinnamon stick, star anise, and bay leaf, and cook until fragrant, stirring constantly, about 1 minute.

2. Add the cayenne pepper, onion, garlic, and ginger. Cook for 1 minute, then stir in the tomatoes and bell pepper.

3. Add the rice and cook for 2 minutes, stirring constantly, then add the vegetable stock and coconut milk, and season with salt and pepper. Bring the stock to a boil, cover (see Tip on page 130), reduce the heat to low, and simmer until the rice is tender and has absorbed all of the liquid, 20 minutes.

4. Remove the cinnamon stick, star anise, and bay leaf from the pot. Stir in the cashews before serving.

# ATASSI
## Beninese Rice and Beans

SERVES 6

**SOAKING TIME:** 8 hours ✦ **PREP TIME:** 5 minutes ✦ **COOK TIME:** 45 minutes

*Atassi is a very popular specialty of Benin and Togo. It's called atassi in the south in the Fongbe language, watché in the north in the Dendi language, and ayimonlou in Togo.*

9 ounces (255 g) black-eyed peas or red beans

3 cups (600 g) white rice

½ teaspoon ground cumin

½ teaspoon paprika

1½ tablespoons baking soda

Salt

1. Soak the black-eyed peas in 3 cups (720 ml) water for at least 8 hours. Rinse and drain, then place them in a large pot with 5 cups (1.2 L) water. Bring the water to a boil, cover the pot, and cook the beans over medium heat until tender, 20 minutes.

2. Add the rice, cumin, paprika, and salt to the pot. Stir well, add the baking soda, and stir again. Cook over medium heat for 5 minutes, then reduce the heat to low.

3. Cook until the rice is tender, 20 minutes (see Tip on page 130). Stir regularly, and don't hesitate to add a splash of water if the mixture starts to stick.

# DESSERTS

# MANGO-CHILE COMPOTE

SERVES 2

**PREP TIME:** 10 minutes ✦ **COOK TIME:** 10 minutes

*This sweet and spicy compote is a breeze to make. It's also a great way to use up overripe fruit. Served with coconut yogurt, it's a delicious, healthy dessert.*

1 ripe mango, peeled and chopped

¼ cup (45 g) coconut sugar

Juice of 1 lime

1 teaspoon vanilla extract

Pinch of crushed red pepper flakes

1. Place the mango in a small pot with the sugar, lime juice, vanilla, red pepper flakes, and ¼ cup (60 ml) water.

2. Let cook on low heat until reduced, 10 minutes. Stir occasionally to prevent the mango from sticking to the bottom. Let cool and enjoy.

# CHILLED MANGO-BASIL SOUP

SERVES 4

**PREP TIME:** 5 minutes

*This dessert reminds me of mango season in Côte d'Ivoire. In the villages, the trees get so heavy with fruit that it's easy to get bored with mangoes. You have to find creative ways to prepare and eat them. One of my favorite ways is simply as a chilled, sweet soup. It's so fresh and refreshing!*

4½ cups (500 g) frozen mango chunks

5 fresh basil leaves

3 mint leaves

2 teaspoons vanilla sugar (see Tip)

Juice of 1 lime

Zest of 1 lime

Place the mango, basil, mint, vanilla sugar, lime juice, and lime zest in a blender. Blend until smooth. Serve cool.

**TIP:** *To make your own vanilla sugar, place a vanilla bean in sugar in an airtight container to infuse.*

# COCONUT-LEMONGRASS MUFFINS

MAKES 9 MUFFINS

**PREP TIME:** 10 minutes ✦ **COOK TIME:** 25 minutes

*Cakes and muffins are very common snacks in West Africa. They are often homemade, but sometimes we buy them from street vendors. There are so many different flavors! This is a pairing of lemongrass and coconut. For a richer flavor, add a square of vegan white chocolate in the center of each muffin before baking.*

½ cup (120 ml) coconut oil, plus more for oiling the pan

⅓ cup (60 g) coconut sugar

½ cup (120 ml) almond milk

1 teaspoon ground cinnamon

1 teaspoon chopped lemongrass (fresh or frozen)

1 teaspoon lime zest

1 teaspoon vanilla extract

½ cup (50 g) unsweetened shredded coconut

1½ cups (205 g) all-purpose flour

3 teaspoons baking powder

1. Preheat the oven to 350°F (180°C). Oil a 9-cup muffin pan.

2. Whisk the oil and sugar together in a large bowl, then add the milk, cinnamon, lemongrass, lime zest, and vanilla. Stir in the shredded coconut.

3. Mix the flour and baking powder together in a bowl. Stir them into the wet ingredients and mix well to form a smooth batter.

4. Fill 9 cups of the muffin pan with the batter.

5. Bake the muffins in the oven for 25 minutes or until a tester inserted into the center of a muffin comes out clean. Serve warm or at room temperature.

# CHOCOLATE MOUSSE

**PREP TIME:** 15 minutes ✦ **REST TIME:** 3 hours

*Côte d'Ivoire is the world's primary cacao producer. There's a good chance that the chocolate you're using in this recipe originated there! Try to choose fair trade chocolates to support local suppliers. This is all the more important for me, since most of the adults in my mother's village, in the center of Côte d'Ivoire, are involved in cacao production.*

1½ ounces (45 g) dark chocolate

2 avocados

¼ cup (60 ml) coconut milk

⅓ cup (80 ml) agave nectar

⅓ cup (30 g) unsweetened cacao powder

2 teaspoons vanilla extract

Pinch of sea salt

Chocolate chips

Fresh fruit

Granola

1. To melt the chocolate in a double boiler, place the chocolate in a small glass or metal bowl. Bring a small pot of water to a boil, and then place the bowl on top. (The bowl must not touch the hot water.) Use a rubber spatula to stir and spread the chocolate until it is melted and smooth. Let it cool for 5 minutes but don't let the chocolate reharden.

2. Place the melted chocolate, avocado, coconut milk, agave, cacao powder, vanilla, and salt in a food processor. Process until smooth and creamy, then transfer to 4 small bowls.

3. Chill for at least 3 hours or ideally overnight.

4. Top the mousse with chocolate chips, fresh fruit, and/or granola.

# COCONUT RICE PUDDING

SERVES 4

**PREP TIME:** 5 minutes ✦ **COOK TIME:** 35 minutes

*I was never a fan of rice pudding until I began cooking for myself. This coconut milk rice pudding has won first place with me! You can add golden raisins, almond flakes, or grated coconut to this dish for added flavor. Either way, it's delicious!*

4 cups (960 ml) coconut milk

¼ cup (45 g) coconut sugar

1 teaspoon ground nutmeg

1 vanilla bean, scraped

Pinch of salt

½ cup (100 g) short-grain white rice

1. Place the coconut milk, sugar, nutmeg, vanilla, and salt in a small pot.

2. Add the rice and stir, then cook on low heat until the rice is tender, 35 minutes. Stir frequently to prevent the rice from sticking to the bottom. Let cool before serving.

# BANANA–PEANUT BUTTER ICE CREAM

SERVES 2

**PREP TIME:** 10 minutes

*This recipe is a nod to one of my favorite childhood snacks, yogurt grotto, which is a frozen yogurt dessert eaten on a wooden stick. I was fond of them when I was little. With this recipe, it's easy to make ice cream with no dairy. You can add berries, roasted coconut, chocolate chips . . . let your imagination run wild!*

2 frozen bananas, sliced

1 tablespoon peanut butter

½ cup (120 ml) plant milk (coconut, almond, soy)

Place the bananas and peanut butter in a blender. With the blender running, slowly add the milk and blend until the ice cream is firm but creamy.

# CHOCOLATE-GINGER MUFFINS

MAKES 8 MUFFINS

**PREP TIME:** 10 minutes ✦ **COOK TIME:** 25 minutes

*Ginger and chocolate is one of my favorite flavor combinations. I think you'll love it, too. These muffins are delicious with a glass of Date-Infused Cashew Milk (page 156).*

⅔ cup (160 ml) coconut oil, plus more for oiling the pan

¾ cup plus 2 tablespoons (160 g) coconut sugar

⅔ cup (160 ml) plant milk

¾ cup plus 1 tablespoon (75 g) unsweetened cacao powder

1 teaspoon vanilla extract

¾ cup plus 1 tablespoon (150 g) crystallized ginger, coarsely chopped

1½ cups (205 g) all-purpose flour

2 teaspoons baking powder

2 teaspoons baking soda

2 teaspoons apple cider vinegar

1. Preheat the oven to 350°F (180°C). Oil an 8-cup muffin pan.

2. Whisk the oil and sugar together in a large bowl. Add the milk, cacao powder, vanilla, and ginger, and mix well.

3. Mix the flour, baking powder, and baking soda together in a bowl. Stir them slowly into the wet mixture and combine well to form a smooth batter.

4. Fill 8 muffin cups of the muffin pan with the batter.

5. Bake the muffins in the oven for 25 minutes or until a tester inserted into the center of a muffin comes out clean. Serve warm or at room temperature.

# PEANUT-DATE COOKIES

MAKES 12 COOKIES

**PREP TIME:** 10 minutes ✦ **CHILL TIME:** 15 minutes ✦ **COOK TIME:** 10 minutes

*Cookies were probably the first desserts I learned to make as a child. These cookies reflect the flavors of the Sahel with the addition of dates and peanut butter.*

1½ cups (205 g) all-purpose flour

½ cup (90 g) coconut sugar

1 teaspoon baking soda

Pinch of salt

½ cup (120 ml) plant milk

½ cup (130 g) peanut butter

1 teaspoon vanilla extract

⅓ cup (50 g) peanuts, roasted and chopped

2 Medjool dates, pitted and coarsely chopped

1. Whisk the flour, sugar, baking soda, and salt together in a large bowl. Make a well in the center. Combine the milk, peanut butter, and vanilla together in a medium bowl. Stir the wet ingredients carefully into the well in the dry ingredients until the batter is smooth.

2. Add the peanuts and dates. Keep stirring until all the ingredients are well mixed and the dough sticks together. Let chill in the fridge for at least 15 minutes.

3. Meanwhile, preheat the oven to 400°F (200°C). Line a baking sheet with parchment paper.

4. Form the dough into 12 equal balls and place them on the prepared baking sheet. Bake for about 10 minutes, until the cookies are lightly browned. They will firm up as they cool.

# PLANTAIN PANCAKES

MAKES 8 PANCAKES

**PREP TIME:** 10 minutes ✦ **COOK TIME:** 2 minutes per pancake

*These pancakes should be eaten hot, sprinkled with coconut sugar or with a bit of peanut butter. They're delightful!*

1 ripe plantain

1 cup plus 2 tablespoons (150 g) all-purpose flour

1 teaspoon baking powder

⅓ cup plus 1 tablespoon (95 ml) almond (or oat) milk

1 tablespoon coconut oil

1. Mash the plantain with a fork in a large bowl. Mix in the flour and baking powder. Slowly incorporate the milk and oil, stirring to form a thick batter.

2. Heat a nonstick skillet over medium heat. Scoop two large spoonfuls of batter onto the skillet to form a pancake. Cook on one side to brown, for about 1 minute. Flip the pancake when bubbles form on the surface and cook on the other side to brown, about 1 minute. Remove from the pan when browned. Repeat with the remaining batter and serve warm.

# COCONUT-LIME FRENCH TOAST

### SERVES 4

**PREP TIME:** 5 minutes  ✦  **COOK TIME:** 6 minutes per slice

*This delightful brioche French toast can also be made with leftover Sweet Bread (page 41)*
*or even leftover Coco Bread (page 43).*

1 cup (240 ml) coconut milk

Juice of 1 lime

2 tablespoons coconut sugar

2 teaspoons vanilla sugar (see
 Tip on page 136)

Pinch of ground nutmeg

1 tablespoon coconut oil

8 slices vegan brioche

Zest of 1 lime

1. Mix the coconut milk, lime juice, 1 tablespoon of the coconut sugar, the vanilla sugar, and nutmeg together in a wide, deep bowl.

2. Heat the oil in a nonstick pan over medium heat. Soak the brioche slices in the coconut milk mixture on both sides, then cook the in the pan until golden, 2 to 3 minutes per side. Sprinkle with the remaining 1 tablespoon of coconut sugar, just before flipping. Add the lime zest and enjoy while hot.

# DRINKS

# DATE-INFUSED CASHEW MILK

MAKES 2½ CUPS (600 ML)

**SOAKING TIME:** 12 hours ✦ **PREP TIME:** 10 minutes

*Côte d'Ivoire is one of the world's largest cashew exporters, so I grew up eating lots of cashews.
This nut milk is smooth and pleasant, with a light and sweet flavor.*

¾ cup (100 g) cashews
5 Medjool dates, pitted
Pinch of ground nutmeg
Pinch of salt

1. Soak the cashews in water for 12 hours or overnight.

2. Rinse and drain the cashews and place them in a food processor or blender. Add 2½ cups (600 ml) water, the dates, nutmeg, and salt. Blend on high speed until the ingredients are well combined. Strain through a cheesecloth or a fine-mesh strainer.

3. Serve immediately or store in an airtight container in the fridge for 2 days.

# SPICED HOT CHOCOLATE

SERVES 2

**PREP TIME:** 10 minutes ✦ **COOK TIME:** 10 minutes

*This hot chocolate is a real comfort. It can also be served cold, at any time of the year.*

2 cups (480 ml) rice milk

1 ounce (30 g) dark chocolate, broken into small pieces

1 tablespoon coconut sugar

Pinch of ground allspice

⅓ cup plus 1 tablespoon (95 ml) coconut milk

1. Bring the rice milk to a boil in a small pot.

2. Lower the heat, then add the chocolate, sugar, and allspice. Whisk until the chocolate has melted. Add the coconut milk and whisk again. Enjoy warm or cold.

# COCONUT-MANGO
# MILKSHAKE

SERVES 2

**PREP TIME:** 5 minutes

*This milkshake is another nod to yogurt grotto (see page 145), one of my favorite childhood treats. You can replace the mango with any seasonal fruit, such as bananas or peaches.*

3 mangoes, peeled and chopped

2 cups (480 ml) coconut milk

¼ cup (50 g) coconut sorbet

1 vanilla bean, scraped

Pinch of ground ginger

Place the mangos, milk, sorbet, vanilla, and ginger in a blender and blend on high until smooth, 2 minutes. Pour into glasses and enjoy immediately.

# BASIL BISSAP
## Hibiscus Tea with Basil

SERVES 4

**PREP TIME:** 5 minutes ✦ **COOK TIME:** 20 minutes ✦ **CHILL TIME:** 3 hours

*Bissap, or hibiscus juice, is a drink made from dry Guinea sorrel, also called roselle. This is the defining drink of my childhood. Very popular throughout West Africa, it has only been dethroned recently by processed store-bought drinks. But no party is complete without bissap, which can take on many different flavors, depending on region or family recipe. It's delicious with vanilla, ginger, mint, or pineapple juice, and also makes an excellent mixer for cocktails, with or without alcohol.*

1 cup (40 g) dried hibiscus flowers (bissap), drained and rinsed

Leaves from 1 bunch basil

Leaves from 1 bunch mint

¼ cup to ½ cup (45 to 90 g) cane sugar (or coconut sugar), to taste

2 teaspoons vanilla sugar (see Tip on page 136)

Pinch of ground nutmeg

1. Place the hibiscus flowers in a small pot with ⅔ cup (160 ml) water. Boil until dark red and foamy, 20 minutes.

2. Turn off the heat and add the basil and mint. Let cool, then strain through a cheesecloth or a fine-mesh strainer.

3. Stir in the cane sugar to taste, the vanilla sugar, and nutmeg.

4. Let chill in the fridge for at least 3 hours. Serve chilled.

# LEMONGRASS LEMONADE

SERVES 4

**PREP TIME:** 5 minutes ◆ **COOK TIME:** 5 minutes ◆ **CHILL TIME:** 2 hours

*Herbal teas were a large part of my daily life as a kid, used as comforting drinks or applied to little cuts and scrapes. My mother passed this passion for home remedies on to me. Lemongrass, a central ingredient in these infusions, had a special place in our Ivorian garden. Today, I roll its long leaves into bundles and store them in a glass jar. In summer or winter, hot or cold, I love to drink this Lemongrass Lemonade to aid digestion.*

2 lemons, sliced

1 lemongrass stalk

Juice of 2 lemons

Juice of 2 limes

¼ cup (45 g) cane (or coconut) sugar

Mint leaves

1. Place the lemon slices, lemongrass, and 8½ cups (2 L) water in a large pot. Bring to a boil, then let cool completely.

2. Strain the lemon water through a cheesecloth or a fine-mesh strainer. Add the lemon juice, lime juice, and the sugar.

3. Stir the lemonade, then chill in the fridge for 2 hours. Add mint leaves before serving and enjoy.

# KINKELIBA-MINT
# ICED TEA

SERVES 4

**PREP TIME:** 10 minutes ✦ **CHILL TIME:** 2 hours

*Also called "long life tea," kinkeliba is a traditional West African homeopathic remedy. It has excellent anti-inflammatory and antibacterial properties. I love its fragrant aroma, which fills up my kitchen when I dip the leaves into simmering water. I never pass up a hot cup of kinkeliba or an iced kinkeliba tea in the summer.*

1 ounce (30 g) dried kinkeliba leaves

Mint leaves

1.  Bring 4 cups (960 ml) water to a boil. Add the kinkeliba leaves and let them infuse for 10 minutes.

2.  Strain through a cheesecloth or a fine-mesh strainer. Let cool completely, then chill in the fridge for at least 2 hours. Add mint leaves before serving and enjoy.

# MENUS FOR
# ALL OCCASIONS

### FOR A ROMANTIC DINNER

Roasted Eggplant with Tamarind (page 49)

Creamy Avocado Risotto (page 90)

Chocolate-Ginger Muffins (page 144)

Basil Bissap (Hibiscus Tea with Basil; page 160)

### FOR A DECADENT SUNDAY BRUNCH

Mango, Avocado, and Radish Salad (page 55)

Roasted Cauliflower with Peanut-Ginger Sauce (page 62)

Plantain Pancakes (page 149)

Spiced Hot Chocolate (page 157)

### FOR A GOURMET SNACK

Date-Infused Cashew Milk (page 154)

Chilled Mango-Basil Soup (page 136)

Coconut-Lime French Toast (page 150)

## FOR A LIGHT MEAL

Creamy Carrot-Ginger Soup (page 71)

Satini Cotomili (Cilantro Chutney; page 11)

Injera (Ethiopian Flatbread; page 42)

Kinkeliba-Mint Iced Tea (page 164)


## FOR A PICNIC

Grilled Vegetable Wraps (page 89)

Mango-Chile Compote (page 136)

Fresh Pineapple Salad (page 61)

Cauliflower Tabbouleh with Pistachio and Lemon Confit (page 63)

Peanut-Date Cookies (page 146)

Lemongrass Lemonade (page 163)

Basil Bissap (Hibiscus Tea with Basil; page 160)


## FOR PRE-DINNER DRINKS AND SNACKS

Peanut Hummus (page 22)

Crunchy Spiced Chickpeas (page 18)

Vegetable Pastels (page 66)

Peri-Peri Sauce (page 15)

Lemongrass Lemonade (page 163)


## TO SURPRISE THE KIDS

Yassa Burger (page 108)

Sweet Potato Fries (page 36)

Coconut-Mango Milkshake (page 158)


## FOR A WEEKDAY LUNCH

Gratitude Bowl (page 114)

Mango-Chile Compote (page 136)

# ACKNOWLEDGMENTS

Thank you to my mom, Marie-Madeleine, who first introduced me to the flavors and techniques of Ivorian and Burkinabe cuisine. You are an incredible source of love in my life.

Thank you endlessly to my husband, Marc, who supported and encouraged me through months of work and research with grace. You pushed me to go even further at every step.

Thank you to my brothers, Desiré and Alexandre, my greatest role models and unconditional supporters.

To my big sister Monique, with whom I will always share my love of cooking. I hope to transfer this love to your little Maëlys.

I love all of you so much. Papa, I love you, too.

Thank you to Fatou Wagué, my friend and photographer who so brilliantly captured my vision in these pages.

Thank you to our models Isadora, Desiré, Alexandre, and Marc. What beautiful moments we shared working on this book!

Thank you to Sarah, our sidekick from the very first hour.

Thank you to Simone and Jean-Luc, my terrific in-laws, along with the whole family in Alsace.

Thank you to my dear aunt Mariam and to my family in Paris, Meaux, Abidjan, London, Nashville, and Ouagadougou.

Thank you to Patricia, Charlotte, Stessie, Jeanne, Clémence, Astou, and all my dear friends who have become my family. Your words helped keep me happy throughout this process.

Thank you, from the bottom of my heart, to everyone who bought my first book in October of 2020. It all started with you.

A special thanks to my editors, Celine Le Lamer and Wendy Gobin, for their trust and support, and thank you to my American editor, Olivia Peluso, and my translator, Kit Malloy, and Kennedy Cassy, who helped me very much in the process.

Finally, thank you to all who took the time to read these last few lines. I hope this book will inspire you, that you'll make my recipes your own and bring them to life.

With love and affection,
Marie Kacouchia

# INDEX

NOTE: Page numbers in *italics* refer to photos.

## A

African cuisines, 1

African Pistachio Stew (Egusi Stew), *98, 99*

African superfoods, 4

Alloco (Fried Plantains), *32, 33*

allspice, *156, 157*

Angolan Peanut Soup (Sopa de Amendoim), *74, 75*

apples, 106

apricot jam, 106

Atakilt Wat (Ethiopian Cabbage, Potatoes, and Carrots), *102, 103*

Atassi (Beninese Rice and Beans), *132, 133*

attiéké (cassava couscous), *64, 65*

avocados

    about, 4

    Chocolate Mousse, *138, 139*

    Creamy Avocado Risotto, 90

    Etor (Ghanaian Banana Purée), *120, 121*

    Fresh Pineapple Salad, *60, 61*

    Gratitude Bowl, 114, *115*

    Grilled Vegetable Wraps, 88, 89

    Mango, Avocado, and Radish Salad, *54, 55*

    Yassa Burger, 108, *109*

## B

Banana–Peanut Butter Ice Cream, *142, 143*

basil

    Basil Bissap (Hibiscus Tea with Basil), *160, 161*

    Chilled Mango-Basil Soup, 136

beans

    Atassi (Beninese Rice and Beans), *132, 133*

    Chakalaka (South African Relish), *94, 95*

    Creamy White Bean Soup with Crispy Coconut Bacon, 72

    Githeri (Kenyan Corn and Bean Stew), 110, *111*

    Red Bean Cakes, 25

    Sweet Potato and Kidney Bean Stew, *96, 97*

beets

    Gratitude Bowl, 114, *115*

    Key Sir Alicia (Ethiopian Beet and Potato Stew), *116, 117*

Beninese Rice and Beans (Atassi), *132, 133*

bissap (dried hibiscus flowers), *160, 161*

black-eyed peas

    Atassi (Beninese Rice and Beans), *132, 133*

    Red Red (Ghanian Red Stew), *104, 105*

Bobotie (South African Casserole), 106
brioche, 150, *151*
brunch menu, 166
butternut squash, 84, *85*

## C

cabbage
    Atakilt Wat (Ethiopian Cabbage,
        Potatoes, and Carrots), *102, 103*
    Red Cabbage Salad with Mango and
        Peanuts, 52, *53*
    Red Cabbage Salad with Mango and Raw
        Okra, 58, *59*
    Vegetable Mafe (Malian Peanut Stew),
        *112, 113*
cacao powder
    about, 4
    Chocolate-Ginger Muffins, 144, *145*
    Chocolate Mousse, 138, *139*
    *See also* chocolate, dark
canned goods, as pantry item, 3
carrots
    Atakilt Wat (Ethiopian Cabbage,
        Potatoes, and Carrots), *102, 103*
    Bobotie (South African Casserole), 106
    Chakalaka (South African Relish), 94,
        *95*
    Creamy Carrot-Ginger Soup, 70, *71*
    Creamy Roasted Tomato and Pepper
        Soup, 68, *69*
    Gari Foto (Togan Cassava with
        Tomato), 107
    Rwandan Vegetable Soup, 76, *77*
    Vegetable Mafe (Malian Peanut Stew),
        *112, 113*
    Vegetable Pastels, 66
cashews
    Creamy Carrot-Ginger Soup, 70, *71*
    Date-Infused Cashew Milk, 154, *155*
    Fonio and Papaya Salad, 57
    Pilau Rice, 131
    Sweet Potato Salad with Mixed Baby
        Greens and Cashews, 50, *51*

Vermicelli Rice with Spinach and
    Cashews, *124, 125*
Cassava Tabbouleh with Radishes and Herbs,
    64, *65*
cauliflower
    Cauliflower Tabbouleh with Pistachio and
        Lemon Confit, 63
    Cauliflower Yassa with Olives, 82, *83*
    Roasted Cauliflower with Peanut-Ginger
        Sauce, 62
celery
    Creamy White Bean Soup with Crispy
        Coconut Bacon, 72
    Rwandan Vegetable Soup, 76, *77*
Chakalaka (South African Relish), 94, *95*
Chapati (East African Flatbread), 38, *39*
chickpeas
    Chakalaka (South African Relish), 94, *95*
    Crunchy Spiced Chickpeas, 18, *19*
    Cumin-Spiced Orange and Chickpea
        Salad, 56
    Peanut Hummus, 22, *23*
    Roasted Sweet Potato Hummus, 20, *21*
Chilled Mango-Basil Soup, 136
Chilled Watermelon, Tomato, and Mango
    Soup, 73
chives, *44, 45*
chocolate, dark
    Chocolate Mousse, 138, *139*
    Spiced Hot Chocolate, *156, 157*
    *See also* cacao powder
Chocolate-Ginger Muffins, 144, *145*
cilantro
    Fresh Pineapple Salad, 60, *61*
    Gratitude Bowl, 114, *115*
    Key Sir Alicia (Ethiopian Beet and Potato
        Stew), *116, 117*
    Red Cabbage Salad with Mango and
        Peanuts, 52, *53*
    Satini Cotomili (Cilantro Chutney), 11
Coco Bread, 43
coconut
    Coco Bread, 43
    Coconut-Lemongrass Muffins, 137

Creamy White Bean Soup with Crispy Coconut Bacon, 72
coconut milk
    Coco Bread, 43
    Coconut-Lime French Toast, 150, *151*
    Coconut-Mango Milkshake, 158, *159*
    Coconut Rice Pudding, 140, *141*
corn
    about, 3
    Creamy Corn Soup with Peanuts, 67
    Githeri (Kenyan Corn and Bean Stew), 110, *111*
    Irio (Potato, Pea, and Corn Purée), 118, *119*
    Sweet Pepper and Corn Cakes, 24
Creamy Avocado Risotto, 90
Creamy Carrot-Ginger Soup, *70*, *71*
Creamy Corn Soup with Peanuts, 67
Creamy Roasted Tomato and Pepper Soup, 68, *69*
Creamy White Bean Soup with Crispy Coconut Bacon, 72
Crunchy Spiced Chickpeas, 18, *19*
cucumbers
    Cauliflower Tabbouleh with Pistachio and Lemon Confit, 63
    Fresh Pineapple Salad, *60*, 61
    Ivorian Vinaigrette (Virgin Sauce), 8, *9*
    Kachumbari (East African Tomato and Onion Salad), 56
Cumin-Spiced Orange and Chickpea Salad, 56

**D**

dates
    Date-Infused Cashew Milk, 154, *155*
    Peanut-Date Cookies, 146, *147*
drinks and snacks menu, 167

**E**

East African Flatbread (Chapati), 38, *39*
East African Tomato and Onion Salad (Kachumbari), 56
eggplants
    Plantain and Eggplant Stew, 80, *81*
    Roasted Eggplant with Tamarind, 48, *49*
    Vegetable Mafe (Malian Peanut Stew), *112*, 113
    Vegetable Pastels, 66
    Yam Akpessi (Ivorian Eggplant and Yam), 100, *101*
Egusi Stew (African Pistachio Stew), 98, 99
Ethiopian Beet and Potato Stew (Key Sir Alicia), 116, 117
Ethiopian Cabbage, Potatoes, and Carrots (Atakilt Wat), *102*, 103
Ethiopian Flatbread (Injera), 42
Etor (Ghanaian Banana Purée), *120*, 121

**F**

fats, as pantry item, 3
Fonio and Papaya Salad, 57
Fresh Pineapple Salad, *60*, 61
Fried Plantains (Alloco), 32, *33*
fruits, as pantry item, 3

**G**

Gari Foto (Togan Cassava with Tomato), 107
garlic, as pantry item, 4
Geelrys (South African Yellow Rice with Raisins), 128, *129*
Ghanaian Banana Purée (Etor), *120*, 121
Ghanian Red Stew (Red Red), 104, *105*
ginger
    about, 4
    Cauliflower Yassa with Olives, 82, 83
    Chocolate-Ginger Muffins, 144, *145*
    Creamy Carrot-Ginger Soup, *70*, *71*
    Nokoss Vert (Senegalese Green Pepper Paste), 14

ginger *(continued)*
    Red Red (Ghanian Red Stew), 104, *105*
    Roasted Cauliflower with Peanut-Ginger
        Sauce, 62
    Sweet Potato and Ginger Loaf, *26, 27*
Githeri (Kenyan Corn and Bean Stew), 110,
    *111*
grains, as pantry item, 3
Gratitude Bowl, 114, *115*
greens
    Grilled Vegetable Wraps, 88, 89
    Sweet Potato Salad with Mixed Baby
        Greens and Cashews, 50, *51*
Grilled Squash with Harissa, 84, *85*
Grilled Vegetable Wraps, 88, 89

## H

harissa
    Grilled Squash with Harissa, 84, *85*
    Potato Stew with Olives, 92, *93*
Hibiscus Tea with Basil (Basil Bissap), 160, *161*

## I

Injera (Ethiopian Flatbread), 42
Irio (Potato, Pea, and Corn Purée), 118, *119*
Ivorian Eggplant and Yam (Yam Akpessi),
    100, *101*
Ivorian Vinaigrette (Virgin Sauce), 8, *9*

## J

Jollof Rice, 130

## K

Kachumbari (East African Tomato and Onion
    Salad), 56
Kenyan Corn and Bean Stew (Githeri), 110,
    *111*
Key Sir Alicia (Ethiopian Beet and Potato
    Stew), 116, *117*

kids' menu, 167
kinkeliba
    about, 4
    Kinkeliba-Mint Iced Tea, 164, *165*

## L

legumes, as pantry item, 3
lemongrass
    Coconut-Lemongrass Muffins, 137
    Lemongrass Lemonade, *162, 163*
lemons/lemon juice
    Cauliflower Tabbouleh with Pistachio and
        Lemon Confit, 63
    Kachumbari (East African Tomato and
        Onion Salad), 56
    Lemongrass Lemonade, *162, 163*
lentils
    Bobotie (South African Casserole), 106
    Rice with Green Lentils and Onion, 126,
        *127*
    Rwandan Vegetable Soup, 76, *77*
light meal menu, 167
lime juice
    Coconut-Lime French Toast, 150, *151*
    Crunchy Spiced Chickpeas, 18, *19*
    Fresh Pineapple Salad, *60, 61*
    Lemongrass Lemonade, *162, 163*
    Peanut Hummus, 22, *23*
    Red Cabbage Salad with Mango and Raw
        Okra, 58, *59*
    Roasted Cauliflower with Peanut-Ginger
        Sauce, 62
    Roasted Sweet Potato Hummus, 20, *21*
lunch menu, 167

## M

Malian Peanut Stew (Vegetable Mafe), *112, 113*
mangoes
    Chilled Mango-Basil Soup, 136
    Chilled Watermelon, Tomato, and Mango
        Soup, 73

Coconut-Mango Milkshake, 158, *159*

Mango, Avocado, and Radish Salad, *54,*
*55*

Mango-Chile Compote, 136

Mango-Chile Sauce, 12, *13*

Red Cabbage Salad with Mango and
Peanuts, 52, *53*

Red Cabbage Salad with Mango and Raw
Okra, 58, *59*

menus, 166–67

Millet with Roasted Tomatoes, 91

mint

Chilled Watermelon, Tomato, and Mango
Soup, 73

Fonio and Papaya Salad, 57

Fresh Pineapple Salad, *60, 61*

Gratitude Bowl, 114, *115*

Kinkeliba-Mint Iced Tea, 164, *165*

Nokoss Vert (Senegalese Green Pepper
Paste), 14

mushrooms

Egusi Stew (African Pistachio Stew), 98,
99

Sautéed Spinach and Mushrooms with
Plantains, 86, 87

**N**

Nokoss Vert (Senegalese Green Pepper
Paste), 14

nutrition, holistic approach to, 2

**O**

okra

Gratitude Bowl, 114, *115*

Red Cabbage Salad with Mango and Raw
Okra, 58, *59*

Vegetable Mafe (Malian Peanut Stew),
*112,* 113

olives, green

Cauliflower Yassa with Olives, 82, 83

Potato Stew with Olives, 92, 93

onions

Kachumbari (East African Tomato and
Onion Salad), 56

Rice with Green Lentils and Onion, 126, *127*

oranges/orange juice

Cumin-Spiced Orange and Chickpea
Salad, 56

Mango-Chile Sauce, 12, *13*

**P**

pantry ingredients, 2–4

papayas, 57

Paprika-Spiced Plantain Chips, 34, 35

peanut butter

Banana–Peanut Butter Ice Cream, *142, 143*

Etor (Ghanaian Banana Purée), *120, 121*

Peanut-Date Cookies, 146, *147*

Peanut Hummus, 22, 23

Roasted Cauliflower with Peanut-Ginger
Sauce, 62

Sopa de Amendoim (Angolan Peanut
Soup), 74, 75

Vegetable Mafe (Malian Peanut Stew),
*112,* 113

peanuts

Creamy Corn Soup with Peanuts, 67

Etor (Ghanaian Banana Purée), *120, 121*

Gratitude Bowl, 114, *115*

Peanut-Date Cookies, 146, *147*

Peanut Hummus, 22, 23

Red Cabbage Salad with Mango and
Peanuts, 52, *53*

peas, 118, *119*

peppers

Creamy Roasted Tomato and Pepper
Soup, 68, 69

Mango-Chile Compote, 136

Mango-Chile Sauce, 12, *13*

Nokoss Vert (Senegalese Green Pepper
Paste), 14

Peri-Peri Sauce, 15

Satini Cotomili (Cilantro Chutney), 11

Sweet Pepper and Corn Cakes, 24

Peri-Peri Sauce, 15
picnic menu, 167
Pilau Rice, 131
pineapple, *60, 61*
pistachios
    Cauliflower Tabbouleh with Pistachio and
        Lemon Confit, 63
    Creamy Avocado Risotto, 90
    Egusi Stew (African Pistachio Stew), *98,*
        *99*
plantains
    Alloco (Fried Plantains), *32, 33*
    Etor (Ghanaian Banana Purée), *120,* 121
    Gratitude Bowl, 114, *115*
    Paprika-Spiced Plantain Chips, *34,* 35
    Plantain and Eggplant Stew, 80, *81*
    Plantain Beignets, 28, *29*
    Plantain Pancakes, *148, 149*
    Sautéed Spinach and Mushrooms with
        Plantains, *86, 87*
    Yassa Burger, 108, *109*
popcorn, *30, 31*
Potato, Pea, and Corn Purée (Irio), 118, *119*
potatoes
    Atakilt Wat (Ethiopian Cabbage,
        Potatoes, and Carrots), *102, 103*
    Irio (Potato, Pea, and Corn Purée), 118,
        *119*
    Key Sir Alicia (Ethiopian Beet and Potato
        Stew), *116,* 117
    Potato Stew with Olives, 92, *93*
    *See also* sweet potatoes
preserves, as pantry item, 3

## R

radishes
    Cassava Tabbouleh with Radishes and
        Herbs, 64, *65*
    Mango, Avocado, and Radish Salad, 54, *55*
raisins
    Bobotie (South African Casserole), 106
    Geelrys (South African Yellow Rice with
        Raisins), 128, *129*

ras el hanout, *30,* 31
Red Bean Cakes, 25
Red Cabbage Salad with Mango and Peanuts,
    *52, 53*
Red Cabbage Salad with Mango and Raw
    Okra, 58, *59*
Red Red (Ghanian Red Stew), 104, *105*
rice
    about, 3
    Atassi (Beninese Rice and Beans), 132, *133*
    Coconut Rice Pudding, 140, *141*
    Creamy Avocado Risotto, 90
    Geelrys (South African Yellow Rice with
        Raisins), 128, *129*
    Gratitude Bowl, 114, *115*
    Jollof Rice, 130
    Pilau Rice, 131
    Rice with Green Lentils and Onion, 126,
        *127*
    Vermicelli Rice with Spinach and
        Cashews, *124, 125*
Roasted Cauliflower with Peanut-Ginger
    Sauce, 62
Roasted Eggplant with Tamarind, *48,* 49
Roasted Sweet Potato Hummus, *20,* 21
romantic dinner menu, 166
Rwandan Vegetable Soup, 76, *77*

## S

Satini Cotomili (Cilantro Chutney), 11
Sautéed Spinach and Mushrooms with
    Plantains, *86, 87*
Savory Mauritian Crêpes, *44,* 45
seeds, as pantry item, 3
Senegalese Green Pepper Paste (Nokoss
    Vert), 14
snack menus, 166, 167
Sopa de Amendoim (Angolan Peanut Soup),
    *74, 75*
South African Casserole (Bobotie), 106
South African Relish (Chakalaka), 94, *95*
South African Yellow Rice with Raisins
    (Geelrys), 128, *129*

Spiced Hot Chocolate, *156, 157*
Spiced Popcorn, *30, 31*
spices, as pantry item, 4
spinach
    Egusi Stew (African Pistachio Stew), *98,*
        *99*
    Rwandan Vegetable Soup, *76, 77*
    Sautéed Spinach and Mushrooms with
        Plantains, *86, 87*
    Vermicelli Rice with Spinach and
        Cashews, *124, 125*
squash, butternut, *84, 85*
Sunday brunch menu, 166
superfoods, as pantry item, 4
Sweet Bread, *40, 41*
Sweet Pepper and Corn Cakes, 24
sweet potatoes
    about, 4
    Grilled Vegetable Wraps, *88, 89*
    Roasted Sweet Potato Hummus, *20, 21*
    Rwandan Vegetable Soup, *76, 77*
    Sweet Potato and Ginger Loaf, *26, 27*
    Sweet Potato and Kidney Bean Stew, *96,*
        *97*
    Sweet Potato Fries, *36, 37*
    Sweet Potato Salad with Mixed Baby
        Greens and Cashews, *50, 51*
    Vegetable Mafe (Malian Peanut Stew),
        *112,* 113
    *See also* potatoes

## T

tahini, *20, 21*
tamarind paste, *48, 49*
Togan Cassava with Tomato (Gari Foto), 107
tomatoes
    Cauliflower Tabbouleh with Pistachio and
        Lemon Confit, 63
    Chakalaka (South African Relish), *94, 95*
    Chilled Watermelon, Tomato, and Mango
        Soup, 73
    Creamy Roasted Tomato and Pepper
        Soup, *68, 69*

Egusi Stew (African Pistachio Stew), *98,*
    99
Fonio and Papaya Salad, 57
Gari Foto (Togan Cassava with Tomato),
    107
Githeri (Kenyan Corn and Bean Stew),
    110, *111*
Grilled Vegetable Wraps, *88, 89*
Ivorian Vinaigrette (Virgin Sauce), *8, 9*
Jollof Rice, 130
Kachumbari (East African Tomato and
    Onion Salad), 56
Millet with Roasted Tomatoes, 91
Peri-Peri Sauce, 15
Pilau Rice, 131
Plantain and Eggplant Stew, *80, 81*
Potato Stew with Olives, *92, 93*
Red Red (Ghanian Red Stew), 104, *105*
Rwandan Vegetable Soup, *76, 77*
Satini Cotomili (Cilantro Chutney), 11
Sautéed Spinach and Mushrooms with
    Plantains, *86, 87*
Sweet Potato and Kidney Bean Stew, *96,*
    97
Tomato Sauce, *10, 11*
Vegetable Mafe (Malian Peanut Stew),
    *112,* 113
Yam Akpessi (Ivorian Eggplant and Yam),
    100, *101*
turnips, *112, 113*

## V

vegan, defined, 2
Vegetable Mafe (Malian Peanut Stew), *112,*
    113
Vegetable Pastels, 66
vegetables, as pantry item, 3
Vermicelli Rice with Spinach and Cashews,
    *124, 125*
Virgin Sauce (Ivorian Vinaigrette), *8, 9*

## W

walnuts, 106
watermelon, 73
wraps, whole wheat, 88, 89

## Y

Yam Akpessi (Ivorian Eggplant and Yam), 100,
    *101*
Yassa Burger, 108, 109

# ABOUT THE
# AUTHOR

———

MARIE KACOUCHIA is a Franco-Ivorian recipe developer and author. Born in Abidjan, Côte d'Ivoire in 1992, to a mother of Burkinabé and Guinean descent and a father of Ghanaian descent.

Profoundly influenced by her parents' commitment to social justice, she devoted herself very early to the community life. After studying literature, marketing and corporate social responsibility at university, Marie chose to go into entrepreneurship, determined to have a positive societal impact. In 2016, she created Paris-Babi, a brand that works to further the education of young Ivorian women.

The same year, she launched Fête Solidaire, a joyful fair in Tenkodogo-Koupéla, Côte d'Ivoire for nearly 200 children. This event is a moment of escape for the children of Côte d'Ivoire as well as an opportunity to teach parents about the importance of education for girls.

This return to her roots started Marie on her journey to immerse herself in her African heritage and explore traditional African cuisines. African cuisines are rich in history and flavor and she was delighted to discover, in particular, the many traditional vegan recipes of Africa. A self-taught chef with a passion for nutrition since childhood, Marie now sees cooking as a way to free herself from Western-centric paradigms and proudly reclaim her ancestral cultural heritage.

You can find her at @thespicysoul, where she shares her African recipes and offers a fresh look at African cuisines.